101

ASSESSMENT
TIPS

ENHANCING
UNDERSTANDING
OF VOCATIONAL
QUALITY

VANESSA MCCARTHY

Queensland, Australia

https://prickly2sweet.com.au/

Cover design by Judith San Nicolas
Typeset in Arial Nova 11/22/24pt
Printed and bound in Australia by IngramSpark
Prepared for publication by Dr Juliette Lachemeier @ The Erudite Pen

 A catalogue record for this book is available from the National Library of Australia

101 Assessment Tips: Enhancing Understanding of Vocational Quality – 1st ed.
ISBN paperback: 9780645658408
ISBN ebook: 9780645658415

Dedication

To all the VET assessors
and compliance champions.

Contents

Introduction
Meet Prickly

Hi, I'm Prickly.

Think of Prickly the Pineapple as your little friend. Prickly asks the questions that people would like to ask – but don't – for fear of looking silly or feeling prickly because they think they should already know the answers.

Now meet Vanessa McCarthy.

As the managing director of Education Compliance Validators (EDCV) and founder creator of the Prickly2sweet™ system, I regularly get asked all sorts of questions about assessment and compliance that feel prickly to a lot of people. This is because the concepts can be a little difficult to understand or relate to.

Many people find RTO compliance content uncomfortable and hard because it has previously been described as compliance-focused. They have been told to do something for the sake of compliance, rather than having it explained and related to their responsibilities or how it can affect their student(s).

I never intended to write a book about assessment tips. In fact, I originally started to write a book about assessment validation. This book is still in draft form, and I am continually playing with that idea. However, I found that the fundamentals of assessment were something that others asked more questions about – before, during and after any validation process.

This assessment tip book has grown from regular posts on LinkedIn where I shared 25 years' worth of professional knowledge and skills working with Registered Training Organisations (RTOs) as an auditor. I have also worked within the vocational industry in various roles with diverse responsibilities.

During this time, I continued to enhance and build on my knowledge by reading many reports, articles and guides created by the industry bodies. These industry bodies refer to the vocational education and training regulators, ASQA, as well as NCVER (National Centre for Vocational Education Research), whose research informs and influences the Australian VET industry, industry skills councils, education departments, both state and federal, and many more. You will see that some of these are directly referenced in the tips and others are referred to in the recommended reading list. Nothing is ever learned in isolation, and without the experiences of others, this knowledge would be theory only.

It is my hope that these assessment tips are a helpful resource for you, my readers and followers, in your journey through the Australian vocational system.

I actively encourage you to use these tips as a course of discussion topics around assessment with your teams.

This book is designed for those with diverse levels of understanding and experience in the vocational sector, trainers, assessors and resource developers. This includes those developing assessment as well as writing, creating and reviewing assessment. Using a range of basic principles and rules of evidence tips for assessment, as well as tips related to common mistakes and non-compliances, I have tried to capture a variety of levels of understanding so that not only best practice but the opportunity to think outside the box is encouraged.

It Is my goal to embrace and encourage innovative concepts, thoughts and suggestions, and share these celebrative ah-ha moments. I hope the material inspires you to improve your assessments, or at least start to question and review what your organisation considers to be best practice. I hope you enjoy this little book, and I thank all of my supporters, followers, colleagues, friends and family for your continual support throughout my journey.

Acronym Crazy

Our vocational system in Australia has had and continues to have so many bodies and standards that we need to provide an acronym key to refer to. Although a great deal of effort has been used to try and provide most references and full details, it is sometimes much easier to use the abbreviation or acronym. In fact, the abbreviation is more well-known than the long title. Throughout the 101 assessment tips, some or all of the following will be used:

Abbreviation	Long title
ARF	Australian Recognition Framework
	(<u>not</u> ready to fly or the noise a dog makes)
AQTF	Australian Quality Training Framework
AQF	Australian Qualification Framework
ASQA	Australian Skills Quality Authority
CRICOS	Commonwealth Register of Institutions and
	Courses for Overseas Students
DESBT	Department of Employment, Small Business and Training
IBSA	Innovation and Business Skills Australia
IV	Independent Validator
LMS	Learner Management System
PE	Performance Evidence – a criterion of the unit of competency
RPL	Recognition of Prior learning
RTO	Registered Training Organisation
SOA	Statement of Attainment
TAE	Training and Education (the Train the Trainer training package)
TAE40116	Code for the Certificate IV in Training and Assessment
TAS	Training and Assessment Strategy
UOC	Unit of Competency
VET	Vocational Education and Training

Due to the changing RTO registration standards, there has been a common theme for the need to check quality and compliance. These checks are based on a process of reviewing the training and assessment resources against the standards of the training package. Assessment is a foundation to the competency-based system and the key element of ensuring a person's competency is measured and recorded.

Assessment Tip #1
Confusion

Why is assessment creation confusing?

Assessment creation can feel a little confusing, un-comfortable and even prickly. There is so much to consider that you would be forgiven if you are con-fused and don't know where to start. Everyone at some stage of their journey to understanding the vo-cational assessment process has felt like this.

Some of this confusion can result from what others have said or what you might have heard. This book was created because of the common questions I have received during my time as an auditor and con-sultant. As such, the focus is on assessment compliance and what constitutes a compliant as-sessment. I found that specific tips have helped others to break down the bigger problem and picture and slowly but surely remove the prickly feeling. So here are the first tips:

1. The first is to recognise the confusion and start with understanding the major points of a quality and compliant assessment. By the way, quality is not necessarily the same as compliant.

2. Your assessment must require students to demonstrate skills and knowledge across a range of environments and contexts relevant to the unit or module. Assessing in a variety of contexts shows that the student can apply the skills and knowledge in other situations and also apply their knowledge in a practical way. When you are writing assessments consider the task/s; the expected outcome and the steps to achieve it (these are benchmarks or expected responses); and lastly ensure you add instructions for the student and assessor.

3. Add assessment criteria; that is, list what the student needs to demonstrate. All competency assessments are to be based or assessed in real-world situations. Most real-world situations have moments where things do not go according to plan, so make sure your assessment reflects these problem-solving or 'what if' scenarios and

issues. This way, you are able to assess the student's contingency management skills. Think also of alternative assessment methods such as a competency conversation or adding a few questions into your observation, for example: What would you do if..........?

Assessment Tip #2
Development

Where do I get assessment information from?

Many in the VET world create and develop assess-ment tools, instruments and materials. When developing assessments, use the information from the unit or module elements, performance criteria and assessment requirements to determine what competence looks like, feels like and can demon-strate more than once. A word of warning: Don't just copy and paste directly from the unit for the ques-tions or the response. Why? Because each criterion alone does not produce sufficient depth or breadth of competency.

The first point to note is that quality assessment tasks are holistic, so you have to think of a task with more than one criterion.

The second point is to think of any task and all the steps from start to finish to complete the task. Before you start the task, you need knowledge, which is based on a foundation of either new or previous experience. This could include a range of environments and will have the specific outcome and evidence of a competent performance. So this is not just performance criteria.

Assessment Tip #3
Individual

Should assessment be group- or individual-based?

Consider the assessment on an individual-person basis. Assessment must always be based on the performance of the individual student. Now don't get me wrong, in the real world not all tasks are completed by just one person; many are conducted and completed in a team or group situation.

If assessment tasks are undertaken as a group, it is important that each student be assessed on each component of the task. Do not assume that because a group of students completed a task, each of them is competent. A common question I get asked is: How do you capture this in a team environment?

The tip is this: First identify the type of assessment methods that can be conducted via a group. Examples of these are role plays, projects and events. If in a role play, make sure you have each student play different roles or include others to participate with clear roles in different environments, scenarios or simulations.

No matter which method of assessment you choose, make sure you capture the sufficient detail in the evidence for each student. Think outside the box and consider video, audio, online, VR and/or reports from online systems. Just make sure the student knows what they are being assessed for and that the assessment covers both the knowledge and skill needed for the unit/units.

Assessment Tip #4
Feedback

When & how is feedback provided?

Assessment feedback. The human element of feedback is valued by teachers and students alike, but rising student numbers are adding to marking workloads, and students are expressing more dissatisfaction with assessment and feedback.[1]

The ASQA requirements of assessment note 'the need to incorporate the provision of feedback to assist in the consistent demonstration of competency as well as evaluate assessment quality.'[2]

Clearly, not only is feedback a compliance requirement, it is also a human need to know and understand how a person is going in the learning journey, using the assessor's feedback on, for example, the assessment implementation effectiveness of tools, instruments and materials. There are also two ways in this communication pathway, both *giving* feedback but also *getting or gathering* feedback.

How can you *gather* assessment feedback?

I encourage all in the vocational sector to investigate and implement innovative and sustainable ways of feedback compliance methods. Try looking for innovative methods of gathering feedback in your organisation, for both internal and external stakeholders. Include oral feedback recording, via voice message or a text. You could also use artificial intelligence to provide statistical analysis on regular feedback online after an assessment has been completed. Consider other ways you could be recording feedback, such as answering a survey verbally, or visually with graphs or polls. Touch screen smiley face polls are even used in industries such as hospitals.

The vocational sector must, at the time of publication, use the quality indicator tool as a method of feedback gathering.

Assessment Tip #5
Don't Copy & Paste

Do you copy and paste the unit from training.gov.au? Why? It is a common misconception that unless you state the unit criteria directly from the training.gov.au website, referencing the performance criteria and number, the 'auditor' won't know it complies with the unit. This practice is time-consuming and it is difficult to maintain accuracy, especially when units change.

Did you know you do not have to do this? In fact, it is not in keeping with the principles of assessment as it makes instructions unclear for the student. I am not saying don't refer to the unit as all assessments that are based on and designed to assess against an accredited unit must include the correct title and code.

Best practice includes identifying the assessment conditions and criteria in which the response to the assessment is to be assessed against. What is not best practice is taking the unit criteria word for word from the unit.

As they are in the raw source form, the units of competency formats or original structures are not intended to be read by students. It is up to assessment developers to ensure assessments comply; therefore, just listing the unit word for word is not best practice in compliance – it is lazy.

Assessment Tip #6
Foundation Skills

> Do assessments have to include foundation skills?

Foundation skills should be considered with the dimensions of competency when developing assessments. So many assessments do not clearly reflect the foundation skills. Some units of competency align performance criteria with foundation skills; whether the unit does this or not, you need to assess the student against these criteria. Do not assume the assessment methods have included the foundation skills. You must really look at them, consider them and implement them so they are also assessed.

Here is a tip: Foundation skills can be aligned and linked within and with the dimensions of competency. For example, if you ensure you have a problem-solving activity then you should include the assessment of the following foundation and employability skills:

- Problem solving skills

- Initiative and enterprise

- Entrepreneurial behaviours

- Gaining and keeping work.

How are you assessing foundation skills? Remember that like any unit criteria, it is important to not just copy and paste the wording. Include a description of the foundation skill in the assessment criteria. Make sure the tasks clearly include the use of skills like reading and learning as well as the demonstration of effective oral communication by talking, collaborating and discussing. Expand what is meant by 'effective' in the context of the assessment. Using descriptive words such as 'clearly' and 'easy to understand' by using basic terms are just two examples.

Assessment Tip #7
Review

When should assessments be reviewed?

Assessment content can be reviewed at any time. Validation timeframes in the national standards for vocational education are a *minimum*. With all the changes in the units of competency that have occurred and will continue to occur, neither you nor your students have the luxury of waiting for an internal validation to be completed based on a scheduled date.

Tip: Look at your current tools for content compliance against the unit based on a risk management plan. Check them against the newest version of the unit when the newest version comes out and before the end of the transition period.

You do not necessarily need to get rid of everything you have spent thousands of dollars or hours on, from a purchased product to the time you spent creating the documents. As the saying goes, 'Do not throw the baby out with the bath water.' Review now, often and always. What is important is to stop waiting for the schedule.

No matter when you review, always record the activity.

Innovation in compliance can help this process to be efficient, effective and sustainable, and it also manages risk. Want to know more? Stay tuned as more is to come in the following assessment tips.

Assessment Tip #8
Mapping – Part 1

What is meant by mapping an assessment?

Documenting the unit mapping process continues to be a key to compliance; however, this unfortunately isn't the case in most situations as most are not done correctly and are substantially based on bias, opinion and judgement. Having a documented mapping that is just copied and pasted from the unit reflecting it as if reading the unit from the top down to the bottom of the page is a waste of time. Doing it like this completely misses the point of linking performance with the knowledge and evidence of competency.

This method of mapping continues to confuse many in the vocational industry. This method, I believe, is also the reason there is much non-compliance as well as a lack of quality in assessment tools, methods and competency-based training and assessment.

Here are two examples:

1. If the performance criteria were mapped individually, the links with the knowledge required (as there will usually be a knowledge evidence requirement that is linked to enable this performance to be competently achieved) are missed. Only picking up the location in the assessment of where the performance criteria is met and not identifying the aligned knowledge and performance evidence at the same time will mean the person mapping the content will be reviewing not just once, but twice or three times for the related content.

2. Not aligning the criteria before reviewing the content might mean assumptions could be involved instead of accurate assurance of compliance. Not having those links identified prior to actual content review results in the missing of criteria.

Assessment Tip #9
Self-assurance

What does self-assurance look like?

Self-assurance in assessment system compliance is essential for the current registered training organisations. So, what does this look like? Here are my tips:

1. Continuously and systematically collect relevant and sufficient assessment data.

2. Analyse to identify gaps in the system.

3. Act on areas for improvement.

Here are the trends I have seen over the years across the sector, both prickly and sweet:

25

PRICKLY POINTS

1. RTOs are unaware of the data available.

2. Old methods of analysis do not provide clear data to make decisions.

3. RTOs are bogged down in compliance processes that are not providing any ROI Solutions.

SWEET POINTS

1. Clarify the data needed to make decisions about the whole assessment system aligned with business vision.

2. Identify and communicate KPIs of the assessment system.

3. Invest in innovative systems to provide clear, accurate and timely data.

Assessment Tip #10
Systematise

How do you systematise continuous improvement?

For an effective process, the assessment review process should be systematised.

Data is the key; however, you have to know a few things about this data to get any real benefit:

1. Know what data you need and that you need to have.

2. Plan on how you are going to collect this data.

3. Understand where the data will be collected from, how it will be collected, the form it will take and how often you will collect it.

Next, the system must show how the data will be collated and analysed. The data analysis should include the review against the preidentified and agreed KPIs.

It is one thing to have data; however, if you don't share it with those who need it, like decision makers and action takers, it might as well stay hidden. Communicate with feedback to those who have contributed to the data as well as those who are responsible for acting on the gap areas.

Doing this once is not enough to make this a systematised approach. The system part comes in the rinse and repeat of the process. Scheduling is very important, and embedding this process into other digital systems makes it even easier.

Here is an example:

Why?

Goal is to achieve a 95% assessment process. What data reveals satisfaction on the assessment process?

Where from?

Students who have completed online assessment.

When?

Requested after each assessment or after third assessment.

Once a student completes an assessment, they receive the opportunity to provide feedback on the assessment process via an email or through a popup on a site.

Assessment Tip #11
Expert/Guru

I am often asked whether you need an 'expert' or a 'guru' to conduct an internal audit or assessment review to ensure your assessments are compliant.

Getting external or specialist help if you are a very small business and doing everything yourself can be helpful. However, you don't have to break the bank to get the feedback you need. You do need to have an open mind. There are available systems that can pick up gaps, identify compliance issues and provide innovation opportunities.

Remember, an expert has an opinion. To make risk management-based decisions, it is data that is needed, not opinion. No matter what you decide, you will need to invest time and money to either get help or install a system to maintain and innovate your compliance system, or both.

Assessment Tip #12
Unpack

The Australian VET system and industry are really good at acronyms and creating easy-to-remember terms of reference. However, the term 'unpacking' units of competency, for example, is one I find rather unhelpful. Unpacking a unit is used to describe the process of pulling apart a unit's individual criteria and reading them on their own to get a picture of a person's competency to complete a task.

If you are unpacking something, even a unit of competency, there are too many variables, different cases, different insides and different content structure. By 'unpacking' a unit, the reader does not see the alignment within the criteria, for example, which knowledge (knowledge evidence) is needed for a specific task (the performance criteria). So instead of getting a clear, holistic picture of a competent person completing a task, you get a piecemeal assessment that continually repeats itself and misses criteria.

I find it far more helpful to look at understanding units of competency as an object that instils feelings. I use pineapples to help describe this concept. As most people will know, pineapples can feel prickly – especially on the outside – just like all those terms of different criteria if you are reading them for the first time. The way they are structured are also uncomfortable to read as they seem all over the place. This can make you feel rather uncomfortable and even 'prickly'.

People can also feel prickly about how assessment tools, instruments and systems can be compliant for respective units of competency.

Just like the outside of a pineapple, what most don't know is how to tell a ripe one, as you don't always know the taste. Knowing the parts inside are very different. Inside is where you find out it has sweet pieces.

It is far more helpful to understand that, just like a pineapple, you don't know what it is like on the inside of a unit by just looking at the outside and not breaking it open. Knowing what is on the inside is how you find the sweet bits. The sweet bits of a unit aren't just the performance criteria. Understanding and knowing how to apply the relationship each criterion has with the other is also a sweet bit. For example, the performance criteria with its knowledge evidence.

Assessments need to reflect the pineapple. The knowledge of how to read the unit can be like knowing how to find the sweet inside the pineapple. Awareness of how the pieces all come together is the secret to creating a compliant assessment.

Assessment Tip #13
Rules

What are the rules for assessment?

Rule of evidence/proof under the rules of evidence for assessments

I am often asked, 'What do these rules mean?' The basic purpose of these rules is so that the 'assessor is assured' and the assessment evidence is valid, sufficient, authentic, current and able to provide proof of the student/learner/candidate competency level.

Here are the rules from the ASQA website, which you can find referenced in the back of this book. I have also added the links and alignment to the principles of assessment as many rules are linked, which can assist in understanding the evidence rule:

Valid – against the unit of competency, which also relates to assessments being valid and fair.

Sufficient – enough to make a reliable judgement, again linked to the principles of valid and fair.

Authentic – the evidence is the student's own work; a reliable assessment will ensure this is achieved.

Current – recent evidence that also is flexible and fair to the student.[3]

If you use benchmarks, then multiple assessors are aware of the standards and agree with what is considered as competent. If you use a standardised template that includes clear instructions, agreed timeframe, location, resources, fair awareness of what is expected, signatures, feedback, dates and declarations, the assessments become fair and authentic.

If you use a system that checks the compliance with the unit of competency and the outcome can holistically map the content to ALL criteria and conditions, then you will be more confident and assured that the assessment system is producing valid assessment and evidence of competency.

Assessment Tip #14
Real World

A compliant assessment system considers the real-world application of the assessment or task the student's competency of skills and knowledge is being assessed against. Don't use the lazy option of massive amounts of theory questions or just copy and paste the performance criteria as your observation checklist. You might think because it is big, it must be a good assessment. Well, I am sorry to say that quality over quantity is always better.

Refer to the assessment conditions at the end of a unit and find out the environment, the context and the resources you need to consider for your assessment. Ensure your tools reflect and include these. For example: In your instructions, set the scene of where the assessment is to take place and what equipment is needed. Also describe a typical workplace environment or situation where the assessment process is to be conducted. Even if the assessment is in a simulated environment, it should still reflect the workplace in the real world.

If the unit states the workplace as a condition, then it is a MUST condition, and the RTO MUST conduct the assessment in a real workplace. A simulation can only be used if the assessment conditions and intent of the unit allows. If it is not identified in the unit directly, check the training package implementation guides for guidance that the unit is originally based on.

It is not only in the instructions that the real world should be reflected. A quality and compliant assessment should include tasks that resemble what a student would be expected to perform on the job. Therefore, your assessment methods need to reflect the learning outcome.

Here is an example of what not to do: Don't expect a person on a food and beverage service course to be writing out an essay on the history of a food type when the knowledge evidence was looking for key features of food and beverage items on the menu. A better assessment would be to have an example of a menu where the student gives 5 key features of the food. This could be gluten free and vegetarian options, a kid's section and specials, as well as those options related to a time of the day, such as breakfast and lunch, and wine that goes well with specific dishes.

Assessment Tip #15
Strategy

What if I add a lot more questions?

Guess what? You cannot hide behind the 'more is better' analogy for assessment sufficiency. The same goes for your Training and Assessment Strategies (TAS). Your 30-plus pages of repetition in a strategy are not a strategy, they are a door stop. Your strategies should be clear, accurate, adaptive to different cohorts and industry-consulted.

ASQA notes that taking shortcuts, like developing a generic strategy from a template and asking an employer to 'sign off', will not be effective and does not demonstrate that the strategy was informed by industry.[4]

Quality RTOs need to meet and engage with the industry representative or body, have conversations and meetings, and engage in any other activities directly related to the content of the training and assessment to build strong relationships.

Examples of this relationship are requests from employers to meet with graduates for potential employment and the use of industry facilities for the placement of students during and after training and assessment. It also includes discussions with employers on their specific needs and the RTO then contextualising the training with the employers' materials, such as policies and procedures, examples of product-in-training materials etc.

Assessment Tip #16
Instructions – Part 1

Aren't all instructions the same?

Understanding assessment instructions is part of the assessment features that can make or break the compliance status of an assessment instrument. Instructions for assessment can be dot points, steps or in sentence/paragraph format. Online instructions could also include a video of the assessor introducing the assessment activities or tasks.

A word of warning though: For the purposes of inclusivity and diversity, ensure you also have a transcript and subtitles so that students can read these instructions as well. When creating or reviewing instructions, please make sure you are clear about the difference of a learning outcome versus an assessment criterion of an assessment instrument.

The *learning outcome* is what is to be achieved.

The *assessment criteria* are what was demonstrated, observed, displayed and completed to achieve the learning outcome.

You should 'MARK' assessment evidence against the assessment criteria.

Assessment Tip #17
Systems

Thinking of the full assessment system can be a little overwhelming; many don't see assessments with regard to the overall quality and compliance system for the organisation. Specifically with respect to the Key Performance Indicators (KPIs) of the business.

Many do not see a connection, which is a massive mistake. The general consensus is that assessment is facilitated mostly after training. The assessor marks them and provides the evidence of a complete assessment tool to an administration officer/team to record the outcome and initiate the certificate. That's that, job done.

What is missing is all the other parts before, during and after this process. What is also missing is the fundamental link with the RTO as a business. Most funding is based on assessment, employment outcomes or completed-assessed students. Compliance links with assessment also occur throughout the student's journey. Here is an example:

Assessment methods should be noted in the course marketing. State if the student will be assessed on the job, in placement and/or online etc. Training and assessment are obviously noted in key compliance tools such as the Training and Assessment Strategy, or TAS. However, student progression will include a review of the number of assessments completed, not just the one type once, or else the dimensions of competency are not covered. There are many other aspects to the assessment system, such as human resources currency requirements and records management, to name only two.

The final step that reflects the assessment is the issuance of a certificate, qualification or statement of attainment. This step has the compliance requirements, where the time between and after the final assessment is noted as satisfactory. The student then receives the qualification. The system is the whole picture of the assessment, not only the actual assessment activity itself.

Assessment Tip #18
Apply

How do we implement the TAS?

Having a training and assessment strategy is one thing; it is another to implement it AND keep it current. Did you know that RTOs have to monitor the implementation of their strategies and practices to ensure training and assessment continues to meet industry needs? So *how often* are you doing this and *how* are you doing this?

The regulatory authority notes continue the engagement and seek feedback about how you have provided training and assessment, including feedback on the resources used for both training and assessment. They confirm the industry's ongoing expectations for current industry skills and knowledge of trainers and assessors. Yes, it takes a community to ensure compliance.

Innovative feedback can include electronic surveys such as Survey Monkey and plenty of other services.

In the world during and maybe post Covid, QR codes can be scanned straight to your feedback collection methods for quick and efficient data analysis, making almost real-time decisions with the current target groups.

Assessment Tip #19
Criteria

How are you writing your assessment criteria? Some resource writers go straight to the headings or elements of the unit of competency and then each performance criterion is a subheading or task. Some have a more holistic approach and consider the task that reflects the on-the-job skills and activities, which then works backwards to link the parts of the unit. Whichever your method, these or another, consider the following:

Essential content – the assessment instruments need to holistically meet the unit of competency or accredited course module content, and the criteria specifically needs to reflect this content. Consider trigger and key words. Consider the relationship between the criteria and understand what is to be covered.

Context – context is related to the industry relevant for the student. For example, the same unit can be used across multiple industries or similar industries such as aged care, disabilities services, individual support and business.

Concrete active verb – actionable verbs are required for the activities that the students need to undertake, such as demonstrating the task skills, knowledge and attributes. Include terms such as implement, apply, demonstrate, communicate, discuss and complete.

Intent of related foundation skills – review the trigger words of the related and relevant foundation skills needed in the unit you are assessing the student against.

Language levels – AQF and ACSF level should clearly be adhered to and considered.

Method assessment – if it is a task, activity, observation, discussion or role play.

Dimensions of competency – the dimensions of competency are the skills and knowledge to complete the various levels and initial task skills, which is to complete one task competently. These dimensions also include task management skills, which is to complete multiple tasks competently. Contingency management skills are all about problem-solving ability and dealing with difficult situations. The final dimension is the environment/job situation in which a student would be completing the activities. Contingency management and environment are often missed in assessment tools, methods and practices.

BONUS TIP – the foundation and employability skills are linked to the dimensions of competency. For instance, the foundation skills to complete a task skill would be the basic reading, writing and oral communication. Task management can be linked to the employability skills of teamwork and self-management.

Assessment Tip #20
Evidence

What is assessment evidence?

As a follow-on from Assessment Tip #13, Rules of Evidence, using other parties to collect assessment evidence 'it is the quality of all evidence collected (including any supplementary evidence collected by another party) that is important to making a sound judgement about competence—rather than the quantity, type and form of evidence, where it was collected or who collected it.'[5]

There is that word again: 'QUALITY'. In this instance the word quality is represented by compliance with the rules of evidence and includes compliance with the standards and principles of assessment.

Collecting evidence of 'everyday performance' rather than ONLY performance carried out as part of the formal assessment process increases the quality and validity of evidence. This is not co-assessment. This is assessment evidence collection.

TIP

1. Be clear about what is 'evidence' and how and when it is to be collected.

2. These instructions are not to be the unit criteria copied and pasted; instead, these are to be interpreted by the assessor into specific work activities and what 'quality' it is to be completed to. Think measures of the work activities to be assessed here as well as time, quantity, speed and accuracy. Establish what is quality in the assessment. Also consider the real-world situation of the individual and from the team aspects of the job, workplace and business level of quality. Quality that is required in the real world is what the assessment outcomes are to be aligned with. If a student completing the assessment is not providing evidence of the same quality that is expected if it were in the real world then the system and process is letting the industry down, and the student is less likely to obtain or retain the job. The RTO reputation and brand would also be

affected if those graduating from the training could not achieve the industry-expected standards of quality.

3. This is a strategy and therefore is to be noted in the Training and Assessment Strategy.

4. Identify if the evidence is to be obtained or gathered in the morning and afternoon as practice can make perfect, or some activities are set for business reasons in the morning. An example of this could be an assessment related to a production line of a product where the steps that need to be assessed are only conducted in the morning before the other processes can be completed.

5. Real-world environment.

Assessment Tip #21
Direct Evidence

What is direct evidence of competency?

Forms and methods of assessment have a specific link with the type of evidence produced.

Let us consider DIRECT evidence. This is evidence that can be DIRECTLY observed or witnessed by the assessor at the time of the performance or demonstration. The evidence is clearly there to see as an outcome of the activity at the time of the activity.

Linking this evidence to assessment tools includes:

🍍 Observation checklist of what is to be observed during the activity with measurable notes such as time, quantity, quality, characteristics and features of the satisfactory achievement.

🐚 Workplace performance of a task with a measurable outcome. For example, a practical exercise with a competency conversation.

🐚 Challenge assessment. This is often called a 'test', which can create anxiety and a pass-and-fail attitude. Again, this could be a practical task, such as move a forklift to pick up an object.

TIP

Tools for assessment include the recording of evidence. Both an assessor and participant need to be clear on the type of evidence that is being collected, including when, where and how much.

Using only one type of evidence will not provide sufficient evidence of the dimensions of competency needed to make a valid judgement.

Different methods of assessment produce different evidence and different dimensions of competency.

Assessment Tip #22
Indirect Evidence

What is indirect evidence of competency?

Indirect evidence of competency is not immediately available at the time of the assessment in its entirety but is collected over time. This includes things like finished products, written assignments, projects or a portfolio of previous work performed. Some of this could also include direct evidence if the process and task was observed during the assessment process; however, the final product is not at the same time.

Although the various types or one type of evidence are not more important than another, it is the complete set of evidence gathered from a range of points that is important. All evidence of competency MUST meet the rules of evidence as per the guidance set out by the vocational regulator.

TIP

Check the foundation skills to help guide the types of assessment and evidence to gather.

Check the conditions of assessment at the end of a unit of competency to help guide the assessment methods.

Some Performance Evidence (PE) provides guidance on the number of times and types of activities that are to occur; for example, in the unit CHCECE007, the criteria include the need for activities, outlined in the unit, to be completed during a period of at least 120 hours of work in at least one regulated education and care service.6

Evidence of this could include work placement recording of activities while working in a workplace location. It is important to note the need to record the dates and specific location. This unit also notes that competency 'MUST BE' demonstrated in a regulated education and care service; additionally, simulations and scenarios must be used.

Assessment Tip #23
Mapping – Part 2

Is there an easier way to map? It's too hard.

Traditionally, mapping against the unit was and has been a manual process to identify where evidence of compliance is noted in the assessment tools. Mapping may also be used to reflect how other resources such as delivery and training meet or reflect the unit content.

There is mainly one reason to do this: It is for an auditor during the audit of registration compliance and compliance performance for self-assurance. If mapping activities do not reflect the relationships between the criteria, it is just a waste of time.

Do a check on your compliance process and calculate the Return on Investment (ROI). Make sure that you as an RTO know how much the process costs, just like the process of marketing, the process of venue hire and the process of enrolment.

Compliance is a process that has a wide risk reach. Compliance should therefore not be an investment sinkhole. Remember the standards are a minimum benchmark – strive for quality excellence then compliance will be an outcome. Start measuring the mapping process cost by working out the number of people required multiplied by the time they take and how much they cost per hour (wages/consulting fee) to work out your cost of mapping the manual way. There is an even easier way by using the ROI calculator on the Prickly2sweet™ site at:

www.prickly2sweet.com.au

Assessment Tip #24
TAS

What is a TAS?

A training and assessment strategy (TAS) must be unique and identify the assessment methods per course/training product/program, be it a full qualification or just one unit of competency. The biggest problem I have seen with TAS documents is that they are written for an audit. They are jam-packed full of verbose document information and do not contain any flow or actual strategy. Remember a TAS does not mean you have to continually repeat the units it includes over and over in the one document.

The strategy is a document that reflects the original methods of training and assessing a specific cohort. It can also be altered and used for future planning and strategic review of the course/training product. It must reflect the actual outcome and intent of the complete product, whether it is one or many units, a statement or a full qualification. The RTO should include measures of quality in the TAS, how the RTO knows if the strategy produced a quality outcome and milestones with monitoring points.

Focusing on assessment here, the TAS is to clearly identify the way the organisation and team of stakeholders plan to conduct an assessment. It's important to note that this plan must also be evidenced in completed assessments. This means if the strategy says the assessments are going to be done one way or another, there must be evidence of this occurring.

A strategy must be documented, detailed and refer to other system processes and policies related to training and assessment. It does not need to include the source information for everything. This is especially relevant to those processes that are generic and the same for each training product. An example of this is the methods of maintaining human resource currency. If the RTO is maintaining human resource currency the same way across the organisation no matter which training product they are involved in, then refer to the one process.

Specific information directly related to the training and assessment must be included. Again, looking at our human resource example as we did before, in this case specific trainers are to be noted in each training product TAS and could be identified down to the unit of competency level if required.

Assessment Tip #25
Quality

How do you measure assessment quality?

In the VET sector, the RTO national standards specify what a quality assessment is. Principles of assessment and rules of evidence to be followed also assist to provide a quality outcome. Our industry is measured, in part, from the schooling system, which has its own understanding of assessment quality. This may and sometimes does differ from the VET sector.

Consider the following from the 'Teachers' Guide to Assessment'. Keep in mind the similarities of this guide and its understanding of quality assessment as:

1. having strong validity and reliability.

2. allowing opportunities for students to show the extent of their learning.

3. being designed with the learners, the learning goals, curriculum outcomes and the teaching in mind.[7]

POINT & TIP

If we have a lifelong learning pathway that includes a common understanding of 'quality' assessment then our VET assessment quality should be an enhancement of previous experience, not a watering down.

A learning needs analysis and a competency conversation at the beginning is important so that all learning, development and assessment is based on a known foundation of understanding and experience. Inductions or come-and-try days are great ways of informally assessing if the student is suitable for the program. It also indicates if the student has some understanding of the context, complexity and attitude or work ethic that is needed.

An awareness of the students' commitment levels and their time and effort, including the evidence of competency from the assessment, will also assist in setting each student up for success and enhance the quality of the assessment methods and outcomes.

Assessment Tip #26
Tools vs Instruments

Are tools & instruments different?

I have been asked, 'What is the difference between an assessment tool and an assessment instrument?' and 'Why do you need to know?' A simple way of remembering the difference is that assessment tools are like took kits/tool boxes, and each one *contains* and *includes* instruments.

The instrument is the assessment (documented) activities that support the method of assessment and collect the evidence of competency. You might have three instruments in your assessment tool (kit). Your instruments might include specific methods to capture the different dimensions of competency. For example, theory or knowledge in a written format will

73

capture not only the students' writing and reading skills, it will also capture the students' knowledge of a task. A practical activity could include the foundation skills of working with others as well as technology use and the students' ability to deal with a role in the job/workplace environment.

It is important to note sufficient evidence of competency and collecting valid evidence of dimensions of competency is a compliance requirement of the national standards.[8]

Assessment Tip #27
Assessment Review

What do we include in an assessment review?

Consider the assessment system when reviewing the tools. What this means is to look at the validation process and the organisation's compliance culture, not just the tools and documents used or collected as evidence.

Fundamentally, providers of quality education and training are organisations and businesses. They are in the business of educating to achieve an outcome for their clients, whether they are a private or public enterprise RTO, most are in the business of increasing the potential for employment. For any business to be successful, it must spend some time in planning and reviewing its processes. This includes the need to have both internal and external feedback processes. Without this feedback, businesses either don't grow, so fade away, or grow in the wrong direction.

Review of assessment is a process in this full system that supports organisational growth. Feedback methods for assessment review could include methods such as surveys to consider all aspects of the assessment system. A survey could contain the following:

🐚 Was the assessment task clearly identified?

🐚 Were the assessment criteria clearly explained?

🐚 Did the assessment include what was covered in the training?

🐚 Was feedback given at the end of the assessment?

Assessment Tip #28
Innovation

What is assessment innovation?

Being innovative in assessment is not something everyone who has been trained as a trainer and assessor can achieve. Innovation is more than just creating an assessment instrument, even if they have completed the TAEASS401 through training.gov.au.

The unit TAEASS401 includes Performance Criteria 4.2 Develop assessment instruments to meet the required standard and specific workplace/candidate needs and Performance Criteria 4.3 Map assessment instruments against the unit or course requirements.[9]

Innovation is also more than creating an online or 'e' assessment. Innovation in vocational education and training includes not only online delivery and assessment, but innovatively ensuring and enhancing full compliance across the system of training and assessment.

There are already online learner management and other compliance systems for online policies and procedures. The gap until now has been to include innovation in assessment review and validation. Internal audit records, creation, schedule of audits and storing of completed review evidence are also available electronically.

However, what has been missing is the use of technology in the new system of data analysis for VET compliance against the standards, specifically of assessments. Prickly2sweet™ is now available for this efficient and accurate method of review to replace the expensive manual and inaccurate content review process that is completed during processes such as validation.

Assessment Tip #29
Validation

One of my favourite topics is assessment or assessment system validation because so many people get it wrong. This means they don't get all the information and data that this process is capable of giving an organisation. It might sound a bit strange that I like that they get it wrong. The reason I like it is because once they understand what it could be doing for them and the power of data, it completely changes their world and understanding of compliance.

Assessment validation can be the key point of contact for identifying improvements, yet our industry still sees it as outside the RTO's KPIs.

Education Compliance Validators (EDCV) surveyed the VET industry to understand what they really thought about this process. Here are some of the results:

🐚 40% identify accessing skilled validators as the greatest challenge.

🐚 60% of providers are only reviewing 1 unit a month.

🐚 50% have identified the assessment review process is taking more than 4 hours to complete. This length of time makes it an expensive process; however, 30% think it costs $160 or less, which means less than $40/hr. Interestingly, this is not the benchmark for this service when conducted professionally. If this is what some consultants in VET compliance are charging, it is little wonder it's hard to get skilled validators.

🐚 60% have no idea how much the validation process is costing internally let alone externally. The same percentage are not measuring the outcomes against the KPIs of the business. Is this your experience?

Want to take part in the survey? Then please type this link into your browser and have your say:

https://us19.list-manage.com/survey?u=f70d453658e94f374392cea05&id=267cb62428

Assessment Tip #30
Engagement

How can the assessment reflect the feedback?

Assessment methods need to reflect industry feedback and engagement. This is not achieved by giving the assessment to an employer that your students end up with and asking them what they think. Most validators are not qualified assessors. It's the RTO's job to have a skilled validator. The best way to engage with the industry is to:

🍍 Identify the outcomes you are trying to achieve.

🍍 Have a relationship with industry that works both ways.

'Ultimately this, the process, will ensure that employers, industry and students have confidence in the integrity, currency and value of the qualifications issued by your RTO.' [10]

My suggestion is to consider talking to your industry with clear and easy-to-see data. Identify your current compliance score and areas for improvement so you can specifically recognise what is needed. Ask your industry if the methods of assessment actually reflect real work-based contexts and situations, specific enterprise language, job-tasks, current technology, tools and methods.

Make sure the assessment methods meet industry requirements, standards and licences by including employability skills and benchmarks that reflect the level of competency. Ensure your industry engagement focuses on these instead of being a tick and flick exercise.

Assessment Tip #31
Industry

Who are we supposed to talk to?

To explore the industry a bit more, let's discuss who you engage with to make sure your assessments are industry reflective and not unit of competency reflective. Here are some suggestions:

Industry are people who represent the industry as a whole and may be identified through industry associations, employee representatives, business and organisation owners, service skills councils, industry training advisory bodies or councils, employers and regulatory authorities.

Consider reflecting on your network and the engagement you have with them. Here are some questions you might want to ask:

🐚 Have you ever been involved in an industry focus group?

🐚 Do you know of a technical and subject matter expert?

🐚 Who do you use for your industry engagement?

List your industry contacts and the types of activities and interactions you have with them. Then identify two questions or new focus you could have to engage more productively with them.

Assessment Tip #32
Sustainable

Is assessment review sustainable?

Recording assessment reviews needs to be sustainable to ensure the evidence and history of review is readable and utilised, while also capturing system improvement. Sustainable means that the system review is regular and automatic, while also identifying clear gaps for improvement. It then ensures the improvements are developed with SME and other stakeholder involvement. The assessment review is full circle and sustainable, with sufficient resources to see growth rather than being a bland 'tick and flick' compliance-only process.

All RTOs are required to have a validation process, a plan and a schedule. Most RTOs try to manage validation evidence on Excel sheets or Word files. This makes for a mess; it is not a sustainable system based on data-entry accuracy or a user's ability in record management. RTOs need to keep records that are in order and easy to access for data usage. These records also need to link with the review and improvement. Have a look at the management system you are currently using and ask the question:

Is this a sustainable system that is linked to the assessments and can provide all of this process and evidence in one place?

If not, invest in a system like Prickly2sweet™ that links all the records of review history, outcome, rectification and improvement but also your initial compliance with the unit. This system is so much easier and more controllable.

Assessment Tip #33
Understanding

Is there an easier way to understand units?

Understanding a unit of competency and then creating assessment tools to comply is a complex process. Part of that process and best practice in understanding this is to map your assessment. Manually mapping against current or new units is a very time-consuming and inaccurate process, considering that most newly competent trainers and assessors are still learning to write assessments let alone map them. As mentioned earlier, there is an innovative way of doing this; however, here is the tip to help you no matter which way you map:

Please understand that a unit is NOT to be read from the top down. There are specific knowledge and foundation skills that must be understood before completing a performance task (criteria), which is therefore aligned with specific knowledge. If you think of the tasks a student would complete to identify competency, what knowledge and skills are needed to achieve these tasks? Think of a unit going across a page rather than down a page.

Assessment Tip #34
Process

What are the principles of the validation process?

Assessment validation is a very important aspect of the assessment system in an RTO. So too is the process of checking that the validation process is covering all that is needed to get the most out of the resources you invest into it.

When you are developing or reviewing your validation process, ensure you include and enhance these 6 principles of validation:

1. Transparent

2. Representative

3. Confidential

4. Educative

5. Equitable

6. Tolerable. [11]

Assessment Tip #35
Transparency

What is a transparent validation process?

According to NQC: A Code of Professional Practice for Validation and Moderation 'a validation process, purpose and implication, potential outcomes should be clear and transparent to all stakeholders involved. Enhancing this includes clearly delineating and communicating the approach to implementation and justifying the recommended outcomes, including documentation made available to all stakeholders.'[12]

In real words, clearly write down how the validation is to occur and tell everyone involved about it, including why.

Assessment Tip #36
Representative

What do I need to know about representation?

Validation Principle 2 – Representative

This includes considering both the risk and randomness of a sample of the course/qualification. Previously, it was noted that it was not possible or necessary to validate all unit assessment tools or student evidence. A sampling framework should include the sample calculator identified on the ASQA site. Risk is not included in this calculator so that can be considered using other factors such as contract, size of the cohort and industry risk of safety etc.

Another consideration is the use of an innovative method such as Prickly2sweet™ that can review

95

content against a unit within seconds, meaning you can actually review everything, minimising the risk of noncompliance.[13]

Assessment Tip #37
Confidential

Why is validation confidential?

Principle 3, Confidential Validation, includes several assessment-related document reviews, so it is important to ensure all individual, assessor and student/candidate details are protected.[14] It is important to keep the identity of the stakeholders confidential. Here is how you do this:

1. Use de-identified samples of candidates' work and assessors' tools

2. Give the outcomes of the process in a private, supportive environment.

Assessment Tip #38
Educative

What is the impact of integral validation on assessment?

Assessment validation should form an integral rather than separate part of the assessment process. The outcome, as noted in the first principle, is to be transparent and also provide constructive, quality and quantitative feedback. I hope the following definitions will help to explain what I mean:

Constructive feedback is also known as supportive feedback, which is positive, respectful and focused on a goal to solve an area of weakness. An example for assessment would be a weakness in skills and knowledge.

Quality feedback is still positive; however, it is focused on when it is given so it needs to be timely and sufficiently directed at a present behaviour.

Quantitative feedback is the calculated analysis on measurements of customer/client interaction. Examples are things like surveys, polls and other data that help to monitor and identify how your assessment is performing against your goals. This is where innovation comes in.

The VET industry has always reviewed and captured satisfaction and other 'quality indicator' data; however, when reviewing assessment compliance, it was always only a yes-or-no outcome. Validation requires reviewing a statistical sample of students and analysing consistent judgement, plus reviewing the principles of assessment against the rules of evidence.

This is a great opportunity to make use of some great data that can be captured. Using innovation to do this is where some magic lies. There will be quantitative data such as trend analysis in areas for improvement and both current- and future-focused quantitative feedback. However, using a system that can capture before-assessment use can pick up gaps in content before the student even sees the assessment. This quantitative feedback can be used efficiently and effectively by SME to ensure compliance. Establishing the goals of a compliance score and monitoring these can also assist in integral assessment validation.

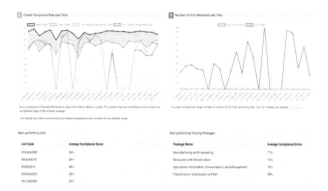

To enhance this principle in the process is to include:

1. The opportunity for industry and organisations to monitor and reflect on their own practice (consider Actual Compliance Scores);

2. The rationales behind recommendations for alterations and/or adjustments are made explicit to assessors;

3. Recommendations for improvement to the assessment tool and/or decision-making process are succinct, constructive, and explicit; and

4. Professional development to support assessors.[15]

Assessment Tip #39
Equitable

Isn't all validation the same, and fair?

The equitable principle is important in the compliance culture of an RTO. Validation policy and procedures must ensure that all processes are demonstrably fair, equitably applied and unbiased.

This principle can be enhanced if:

1. 'Confidentiality of evidence can be assured.

2. The process is sensitive to assessor and candidate diversity and has no inherent biases.'[16]

TIP

Once again, this is another reason for involving an innovative system. The security processes of SAAS systems need to be considered, ensuring confidential login details. Additionally, innovation processes can benefit as there is no judgement or opinion. How are you ensuring no bias or judgement in your validation process?

Assessment Tip #40
Tolerable

How do you ensure evidence variations are compliant?

Assessment variation can occur in the way in which evidence is gathered and interpreted against the standards.[17]

Validation enables the variation of acceptable evidence to be identified and limited to what is tolerable. The tolerable compliance score benchmarks should be identified to measure the outcome. What is tolerable? Tolerable depends on your RTO and their compliance and quality goals.

I recommend that my private clients and our subscribers have an outcome between 90–95% compliance. This is not to be confused with the student's assessment mark or graded outcome. The tolerable score is compliance with the unit criteria. Some units provide variation and alternatives such as options of 'and/or', 'three of the following...', and therefore this will vary between RTOs for the same unit and the context of their delivery and assessment, cohort and situation.

This principle can be enhanced if:

1. Benchmark samples of each assessment method are used as points of reference.

2. Exemplar tools are made available to assessors as well as validators.

3. A risk assessment has been undertaken of the implications of the following: A false-positive judgement – assessing someone as competent when in actual fact they are not yet competent. A false-negative judgement – assessing someone as not yet competent when in actual fact the person is competent.

This is as important to consider as the rectification and remediation.

Assessment Tip #41
Assessment Planning

What's the difference between training & assessment planning?

Training plans are common in VET. It seems easier for numerous VET professionals to think about facilitation and sharing knowledge than assessment and assessment planning. Planning assessment is just as important. Often the training and assessment strategies are inclusive of both areas, so what does an assessment plan have to contain?

Consider the key features, factors and characteristics of any plan:

How, what, when, where, why and who are all key elements of a successful plan. When it comes to planning assessments, all of these are to be based on the outcomes of the unit of competency for those assessments based on an accredited outcome. If not, then consider an appropriate standard.

Also consider BOTH assessment EVIDENCE needed, guided by the rules of evidence, and the best aligned assessment METHOD, covering the principles of assessment.

These rules and principles are more often than not mostly captured in the assessment. Successful, compliant and quality assessments differ in that they are also capturing and clearly articulating the dimensions of competency in the assessment. The dimensions of competency are those that focus on the task, task management, environment and contingency management skills. To capture these, I suggest you start by looking at the foundation and employability skills based on workplace tasks that can then be written in the assessment tools and instruments.

Assessment Tip #42
Tools

Every assessment tool is to include all of the following:

Assessment instruments – assessment methods and the actual tasks/activities/questions.

AND

Clear instructions – including the timeframe, materials, feedback activities and recording of the outcome.

The assessor versions need to include benchmarks or marking guide information to ensure all assessors are making the consistent, reliable judgement across

111

multiple assessments to decide whether a candidate is competent.

TIP

What you won't find in all the assessment development guides is the following tip:

Make sure you clearly identify the actual assessment activity with a unique structure, such as a numeric setting, PLUS identify the assessment criteria. This will also make sure the student and assessor can refer to the activity. Many assessors number theory assessments. Identify the projects/case studies and practicals too. Make sure you can use Parts 1 or A if it is separated. Not doing this can lead to confusion of what is required.

Assessment criteria helps to identify what the student will be assessed for.

Preface this with students must 'demonstrate...' 'provide examples of....' 'will be assessed for...'

Assessment Tip #43
Industry Questions

What questions can you ask when reviewing assessment?

It can feel like you are reinventing the wheel when you are writing assessments. Many have asked me, 'Why can't the regulator just come up with an agreed assessment that is used and accepted by all in the industry?'

There are many opinions to answer that question. The majority are related to the facts that there is too much variation even in one industry and there are some nationally agreed outcomes that the units of competency identify. Some industries do have a national assessment, as in the example of high-risk licences. The problem with these though is they might meet the industry legislation, yet they still don't meet all the requirements of the unit of competencies.

The best way to ensure everything is covered is for the RTO to include industry in the assessment review. To do that successfully and achieve the right data that an RTO needs is to ask the right question.

TIP

Here are some suggestions for you to consider:

🐾 Are you comfortable employing graduates who have demonstrated achievement through this assessment process?

🐾 Do you think that this assessment process will preserve or improve workplace performance standards in your industry?

🐾 Would an industry supervisor-level position be able to use the assessment tools effectively, and what are the LLN and foundation issues to be addressed?

🐾 Were the actions identified in the rectification table achievable and in line with the industry standard?

Assessment Tip #44
Sufficient

What is a sufficient and evidence-based assessment?

Sufficient assessment enables the assessor to decide about competence over time and in different situations. This is going to vary for each unit, and for some students another opportunity will be needed. This is called 'Adjustment', which will be discussed later in tip #78.

Consider the following:

1. What knowledge is needed to complete the task?

2. What skills are needed for the task to be demonstrated satisfactorily?

3. What attributes, behaviour and other foundations plus employability skills are needed to be included in the demonstration and assessment?

This may comprise three methods of assessment or four alternatives. It might be clustered with other units or singular and may include a competency conversation or be more visual than a written task, depending on your student cohort and your units.

Less might be more. Using a holistic assessment validation matrix will show you the gaps.

The current method of displaying this is mapping. Here I am introducing you to the concept of not only holistic assessment but also the holistic assessment validation matrix.

Holistic assessment is covered more in tips #45 and #61, so I won't steal their thunder. It's sufficient to note this one feature: People do not do a task displaying only one criterion of a skill or knowledge. Tasks are performed together and holistically, so we have to get better at doing the same in assessment, as well as displaying compliance holistically.

Assessment Tip #45
Cluster

Can you make the old material new again?

Clustering units in an assessment should be based on a number of factors:

1. Will it better reflect a real-world work task?

2. Can a training package skill set be used?

3. Does the RTO have these units on scope?

4. Will this holistic assessment save time and money?

What are your thoughts?

It's promo time!

Check out the amazing Prickly2sweet™ system as it can review and create mapping for clustered assessments in seconds. It is not too late to review your tools quickly and easily – you do not have to do things the hard way.

Assessment Tip #46
New

With all the changes in the units of competency, how much of the old resources are you throwing away because they do not align with the units that they were originally developed for?

Thousands of dollars are spent each year on resource purchase and creation. The trick to reviewing, upgrading or amending current resources while still saving money is to make existing resources the best they can be. Note, this includes your human resources. You may have heard the saying, 'Don't throw the baby out with the bath water.' What this means is there is probably a lot of resources that can still be used if they are

119

contextualised. The first thing to do is to find what is different. This can be done through a gap analysis between the units. Training.gov.au does this for you by clicking in the comparison section, noted under the content heading of every unit on competency.

The site enables you to click on various unit formats and includes the ability to compare unit content with other releases of the same unit. It also enables you to compare sections of the unit. Be warned, however, as it is not the easiest content to read. The system has a strike-out method of showing changes and can be quite confusing as both new and old is crossed out.

When you click on 'compare', the training.gov.au system will expand the filter and ask you what you want to compare. In this example we are comparing the unit of TLILIC0016 (NEW) and the unit TLILIC0006 (OLD).

Once you click those data filters, the information of the new unit will show you what was in the old and what is now in the new. I find this can be a bit tricky.

The red is in the new and not in the old.

The **black** is in the old and not in the new.

The example from the same unit as noted above shows there is a lot of new performance criteria that is now in the new unit that was not in the old.

In this example, it is really important to note 2 things:

1. **The learning outcomes are noted as equivalent.** This supersedes and is equivalent to TLILIC0006 Licence to operate a bridge and gantry crane, even though significant changes have been made.

2. **All old resources could be enhanced by including this content and also amending the assessment resources.**

TIP

1. Make sure your assessment meets the new unit with a sustainable review process, including new mapping that is easy and cost-effective. Complete a gap analysis.

2. Ensure the new assessment activities are developed by a subject-matter expert.

3. Don't just change a unit code because training.gov.au 'says' it's equivalent. This last one is critical. As you can see from the example, equivalent does not mean equal or the same.

It also means you cannot provide a credit transfer to a student who produces the old version of a unit into a new qualification or is to be issued the updated code. The reason for this is covered in Tip #87 Recognition of Prior Learning (RPL). Basically, a credit can only be awarded for the same unit, code and title. Everything else is a recognition of prior learning.

Assessment Tip #47
Gaps

Is there an easier way to find gaps?

The last tip highlighted the changes and the gap analysis process that are needed when a unit is upgraded or updated. It is a bit of a time-consuming process and can be a little complex to ensure you are not only checking the unit changes between the old and new but also considering the impact these have on the resources.

I used to have to do this for several clients across multiple units at the same time. A question kept popping into my head and poking me with sharp prickles. The question was this: 'Is there an easier way to just get your assessments reviewed and have a clear idea on what your gaps are?'

Others must have had the same question because they were the ones investing in an external consultant like myself to fix the same problem. Other solutions for the RTO at the time included investing in an internal process issue. This, of course, is a massive endeavour and one that not everyone can afford. Even with those solutions, they too have failed as the organisation often does not have the resources, skills and expertise internally – nor was it their core business goal, which made it a big problem. These ended up being not a solution but just another problem.

Now, at the time there wasn't any other solution. Fast forward to today and after extensive research, development and investment, the Prickly2sweet™ system is now available for this process. The exciting thing about this story: The focused, innovative compliance is making a significant impact in the vocational sector, which is making lives easier and increasing compliance.

Assessment Tip #48
Systematic

One of the key messages noted in the NCVER research by Halliday-Wynes and Misko in 2013 revealed that 'a lack of systemic validation and moderation processes within and between providers and training systems is reducing the level of confidence in the comparability and accuracy of assessments.'[18]

It is now more than eight years later and this is still an issue. So how can organisations ensure they implement systems to ensure you and your team are actively not reducing confidence in assessment quality?

TIP

Stop giving industry representatives all your assessments to read over and tell you what they think. Instead, I suggest you put in place a system that includes scheduled networking to discuss feedback during and after training. Before you go, make sure you preview your assessment with a system that provides actual content gap analysis, measures your compliance score and establishes an appropriate measure of quality. This increases your confidence and ensures you fully understand the gaps.

Your industry will then be more likely to discuss specific issues rather than fill out a mass of paperwork. It is up to the RTO to provide evidence of this process, as it is always up to the RTO for the evidence at audit. If processes such as these become daily or routine, evidence is readily available and easy to identify.

Assessment Tip #49
Difference

There is a significant difference between an RTO Quality Assessment and a Quality Assessment by an RTO; however, many don't know what the difference is.

The Australian National Vocational Regulator, AS-QA's, new focus has included the change of the name and focus of performance audits. These are now called 'Quality Assessments' and focus on assessing provider performance on self-assurance and continuous improvement.

TIP

RTOs, you need to embrace and understand the interaction between your internal practices, systems and continuous improvement. It is your system, and it is up to you to show how it works to provide a quality outcome.

For example, what is really in your assessment system? What process do you implement to consider the industry's/employer's and student's needs? Can you provide a flowchart from each point in the student's journey that shows everyone what data you collect and where it is used, where it goes, stored, protected and how it shows you are improving?

Assessment Tip #50
Confidence

How do you maintain assessment confidence?

Assessment conditions are listed at the bottom of the units of competency. Some of these are suggestions of context; however, they also describe mandatory conditions for assessment, for example:

🐚 details of equipment and materials

🐚 contingencies

🐚 physical conditions

🐚 relationships with other people

🐚 timeframes.

It may also specify assessor requirements. How do you ensure your assessment documents reflect and adhere to these requirements? First, don't simply list them or any other part of the unit word for word at the front of the assessment. It is not required, and it does not make the assessment tools compliant.

Instead, try noting what is needed for each assessment method, task and activity. If it is a practical activity include a list of what you need to complete this assessment and link the 'why' to the actual task/s. Do not forget to note the time it will take; location (on the job or simulation); other people's roles and if specific documentation is to be read.

If these can vary, classify the options to be identified by the assessor and/or the student to reflect the workplace. Other options may include a map of the area or location.

The assessor requirements should be noted in the Training and Assessment Strategy (TAS) as this is still part of the assessment system.

Assessment Tip #51
Workload

What is unnecessary marking?

Is your assessment structure increasing your assessor's marking workload with unnecessary marking?

If your assessment questions are based on one question for each performance criterion plus more assessment questions for each knowledge evidence, you are over-assessing and increasing the marking time.

Reliable and valid assessments are created and documented using a process that integrates required knowledge and skills with their practical application for a workplace task. This is known as a holistic assessment. The process also makes sure the unit's content is not over- or under-assessed. If the unit notes 'over a period' or 'on more than one occasion', it can be documented using a summative log or table, documenting the activity once but recording the times it was observed.

A summary statement and instruction to the student should note the requirements for assessment conditions. There is no need to identify S/NYS against each question; however, you must ensure the assessors can clearly identify feedback for areas requiring investigation. This is also another opportunity to demonstrate compliance.

TIP

Take this time to identify your biggest problem with assessment marking. What is it? Write it down.

Assessment Tip #52
Competent

When do you assess a candidate as competent?

The method and timing of assessment will vary depending upon the assessment strategy, the candidate and the competency being assessed.

Formative assessment is to be completed before and during training, and summative assessment is after training or without any training, such as recognition of prior learning (RPL).

Competency determination needs to consider all points, moments and methods of assessment after all assessments have been completed satisfactorily. A completed assessment is to collectively include all aspects of the unit of competency that can be applied in an industry context. These also have been shown through various dimensions of competency.

It is up to the RTO to have a strategy of how to do this, when to do this and what evidence is collected, collated and gathered to prove the assessment has occurred and the competency outcome was achieved. This is one of the reasons that cookie-cutter tick-and-flick assessment methods just don't guarantee or ensure quality compliant assessments.

A student is not competent until all assessment points are satisfactorily completed.

Consider an assessment system that can provide a clear picture of the content distribution across your assessment methods to help you review not only your tools and instruments but also the assessment system and process.

Assessment Tip #53
Valid

The first step is to understand that there are assessment validity and assessment evidence validity aspects to consider. It's important to know the difference between this principle of assessment and rule of evidence.

There are two parts to making your assessment process valid in accredited VET. The process involves both instruments and judgement. Assessment instruments are developed against the unit/s of competency. The assessment process ensures students are integrating and applying skills and knowledge that are essential to competent performance under the required conditions, including contextualisation.

Valid assessment evidence means that all judgements are based on the evidence gathered using the valid assessment instruments of individual performance.

Checking validity is an important part of self-assurance. A significant purpose of an RTO is the valid process of skills and knowledge. Unfortunately, the system should make sure it is sustainable and not reliant on a person or position.

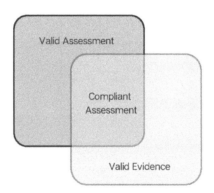

Assessment Tip #54
Fair

Aren't all assessments fair?

The assessment process is not only about the assessment instrument and making sure it meets the unit of competency. For assessments to be identified as fair, the whole process must be considered.

This is from the enrolment process, including a needs analysis and the suitability of the course; making RPL available; adjusting the program that is reasonable to accommodate a student's LLN; informing a student of the assessment process and expectation, timing, context and assessment criteria; having an appeals process and providing feedback.

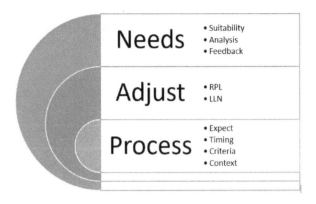

This one principle of assessment alone clearly identifies why it's so important to include more than only a long 'tick-and-flick' process about the assessment questions in the validation process.

The fair assessment principle is one that could and should be included throughout the whole RTO system. Once this is applied, the assurance and confidence in the system is then included in all reviews. This again identifies the need to make self-assurance an important goal of your RTO as it has a huge impact across every part of the business.

Assessment Tip #55
Reliable

Is assessment reliability only related to unit mapping?

The short answer to this question is no. The long answer is that the assessment principal 'reliability' is all about making assessment decisions consistent across different students and different assessors for the same unit of competency. A good system measures variation between assessors and minimises variation through activities such as an independent system review, including benchmark reviews and moderation. Benchmarking and moderation use developed evidence criteria; that is, decision-making rules to judge the quality of performance.

Assessment Tip #56
Evidence Rules

What is assessment evidence?

Evidence is information which, when matched against a unit of competency or module, provides proof of competency.[19] This is flexible for an RTO to determine what evidence is required for a particular competency. There are a couple of things to consider:

1. All evidence must meet the rules of evidence, which are valid, sufficient, current and authentic.

2. Use a variety of evidence; that is, direct, indirect and supplementary.

3. Align with the outcomes of the unit of competency. Remember that not all assessment methods,

and therefore not all evidence, are the best fit for all units and all criteria. Understanding the unit criteria relationships and how they link makes all the difference. If your mapping of an assessment does not do this, you are wasting your time mapping manually.

Assessment Tip #57
Gathering

What is evidence gathering?

When talking about competency-based assessment, the key thing to remember here is evidence gathering. This is the process of capturing all the information, observation, knowledge and skill attributes of a student completing or performing the task. The keys are:

🍍 write it down

🍍 video the activity

🍍 record the response to a set of questions

🍍 gather from a variety of sources

🐾 gather different dimensions of competency

🐾 gather in accordance with the RTO's strategy (TAS).

What you could do is include other people to gather the evidence. It is important to note that only a qualified assessor that meets the standards for RTOs can make the judgement of competency. This is called supplementary evidence, and an example of this evidence is third-party assessment.

Assessment Tip #58
Teamwork

How willing is your assessment team?

Willingness to be part of your validation is very important to the success of an assessment system's processes and significant review.

Validation is to be completed on top of assessment marking, observation and other duties such as training, so can be considered additional.

Our top tips to get your team involved include making it easier for them to dive right in! Stop expecting your highly qualified assessors to want to sit down for hours and discuss something they think already works or have previously provided feedback on. They will want to see that changed first.

Try giving the team easy-to-read data about your compliance status and score. Provide a clear rectification table that shows the areas you need their assistance with, as well as their subject matter expertise and experience. This assists with any new ways it can be assessed, which are right for their students, or to implement changes in the industry.

Make this important process interesting and time-efficient by putting everyone involved at ease. Ensure they understand the common purpose and are having a bit of fun.

This is better for them and better for the business, which means it's better for the industry and better for the students.

Assessment Tip #59
Satisfactory

When do you use C & NYC in marking?

The VET sectors use competent 'C' and not yet competent 'NYC' to reflect the final outcome of assessment. The confusion is when to use 'satisfactory' or 'competent'.

A big mistake RTOs make is using the competent outcome for part of the assessment method. Competent marks or outcomes can only be used when all assessment methods have been completed, as outlined in the training and assessment strategy (TAS) satisfactorily.

Use satisfactory as an outcome of each assessment method, then when all assessments are satisfactory, the student is marked competent overall.

Assessment Tip #60
Foundation Skills

What are foundation skills?

The National Foundation Skills Strategy for Adults defines foundation skills as 'the combination of English language, literacy and numeracy (LLN) - listening, speaking, reading, writing, digital literacy and use of mathematical ideas; and employability skills, such as collaboration, problem solving, self-management, learning and information and communication technology (ICT) skills required for participation in modern workplaces and contemporary life.' [20]

Some units explicitly identify these in a table, sometimes linked to PCs, and some do not.

Finding the trigger words in the unit of competency criteria is one of the easy ways of seeing how you can add this content and skill into an assessment. If you are doing this manually, invest in a highlighter for each foundation skill to see the links visually. Sweet tip.

Assessment Tip #61
Holistic

What is holistic assessment?

Appropriate clustering is a key way to ensure that assessments are holistic in that the assessor can gather evidence and cross-reference it across several units of competency. Clustering, where appropriate, may also result in reducing the time and cost of assessment.[21] A holistic assessment task can consider several criteria within the unit or cluster units together to reflect a real work task. Task knowledge and performance, which also includes a problem, need to be addressed so the student can also demonstrate problem-solving aptitude How many criteria in a unit did you spot in the definition?

Assessment Tip #62
Over Time

Why should assessment be done over time?

One of the biggest problems RTOs find themselves with is a lack of evidence that the assessment was conducted over time, especially when stipulated in the unit's PE. It may not be that the student is not doing the activities, it could be that it is not properly identified as evidence.

For example, a common unit in the Community Services training package is CHCCOM005 - Communicate and work in health or community services. The following points are in the PE, which are to be demonstrated in the evidence of the performance criteria of this unit:

* Three different **work** situations or three different situations,

*..... two colleagues,

*completed two written or electronic workplace documents.

TIP

Look across the other units you are assessing in the workplace and see how the requirements of communication can be aligned. Communication should be incorporated across all areas of the job tasks. Identify how the criterion in each unit also aligns with other units.

HINT

Check if a unit is a prerequisite for other units, which will mean the student has to complete these first.

Assessment Tip #63
Resources

> Don't all assessments occur in the workplace?

Are you making sure your assessments have the resources to complete the activities if they are conducted in the workplace? Although a lot of RTOs apply assessment activities in a simulated environment, there are instances where the assessment is conducted in the workplace. There are two common problems that occur:

1. The simulated environment does not provide a realistic situation that reflects a real workplace.

2. The workplace assessment is conducted by a third-party document.

TIP

To guarantee compliance, you must ensure your review process includes:

1. In the event of simulation, we suggest a complete list of resources in the simulated environment. This includes other people and distractions so it is just like a workplace. These external factors and features need to be evident in the assessment process and tools for each assessment method.

2. The second focus is to not overdo the third-party process. Ensure there are clear activity instructions for both the student and assessor. Both instruction sets should include context, environment and resources. A resources agreement, often required for a funded contract agreement, can work well with the workplace so they can plan what is to be assessed in the workplace with you and the student.

Assessment Tip #64
Purchased

Should all purchased documents be compliant?

Purchased assessment resources cannot be 'guaranteed' as compliant. Even if the resources come with mapping, it is the RTO's responsibility to contextualise the material and content to ensure the mapping reflects this. Having an independent review of assessments and benchmark responses will ensure a clear compliance mapping outcome. The method of mapping and the tools used have been included in the TAE training; however, this is not an efficient or accurate method as it is based on opinion and bias. Only innovation using an online system provides a true nonbiased opinion when reviewing assessment content.

Assessment Tip #65
Involvement

Industry involvement is needed to ensure that all your training and assessment activities are informed of the real-world workplace needs. So how do you do this? It must be cyclic, continuous and impact all aspects of the student's journey.

Discuss aspects such as:

 Ensuring that the training delivered meets the industry needs of employability skills, such as teamwork, and has integrity for employment and further study.

🐚 Ensuring the development and use of simulated environments are informed through consultation with industry stakeholders.

🐚 Providing other feedback including discussion on content gap areas; improvements needed, such as timing, group size, realism and new technology or industry trends; the skills and knowledge of trainers and assessors and all other feedback on the resources used for training and assessment.

TIP

The best thing to do is this: Talk to the industry, meet with them, ask them to be a part of the process, go to the workplace and discuss how the students are doing, follow your students that have completed the course and get involved with contextualising your activities to suit the industry. Don't forget to record the interactions.

Assessment Tip #66
Instructions – Part 2

What are assessment instructions & notifications?

There are some key points, features and structures to be included in the assessment instructions as well as when to notify candidates of the assessment activities, methods and processes.

First is the location of the assessment. Where is the assessment occurring – in a simulated environment or in the workplace? Or does it need to be in a regulated environment; for example, in a registered childcare centre or in a registered food processing facility. Next, ask the following questions to make sure you have covered all the features needed in the instructions to ensure the assessment meets the rules of evidence and principles of assessment:

161

Q1 Resources – Is it an open or closed book assessment task?

Q2 Time – How much time will it take and how many attempts can you get?

Q3 Assessment criteria – What will the student be assessed for; in other words, what are you marking them for?

Q4 Method of assessment – Which type of assessment will it be: written, practical or a combination?

Q5 Other specific task requirements – What other specific task requirements need to be known, such as length of response, and how many times do you have to complete the task? Logbooks are usually the record of this type of assessment instruction.

Please note: You should not copy and paste the unit into the assessment or even place a copy of it in the assessment. One of the main reasons for this is if the unit changes in subsequent versions, you may have to update the assessment. Just provide a link.

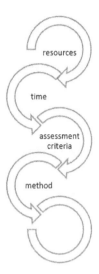

The student version should also include declarations, statement of plagiarism, authenticity process and/or declaration, feedback areas and signatures of acceptance. Refer to other information such as the student handbook or include the instructions in the assessment plan. Authenticity is a high-risk evidence collection area especially for simulated, online and virtual blended assessments. The fundamental requirements for both student and assessor instructions need to be very clear.

The assessor version needs to have separate benchmark responses and examples. Benchmarks are broad-range statements describing competent and satisfactory responses to demonstrate competency. These too should have clear instructions for the assessor and the assessment process.

Assessment Tip #67
Over or Under

What does over- or under-assessment mean?

Your assessment review system needs to clearly identify and define where and when you are over- and under-assessing while noting areas for quality improvement.

Over-assessing is when there is too much assessment, over and above the unit/s being assessed and over the level of the unit needs. It can also include too many assessment methods.

Under-assessing is when there is not enough or insufficient assessment of the unit/s criterion. When content is under-assessed, you are easily not compliant.

Both assessment issues indicate a lack of quality. How do you check if you are over- or under-assessing?

Only a sophisticated and innovative review system will do this for you in minutes.

All other manual processes and systems can take hours/days and a few people.

The key areas should include:

1. A statistical analysis of how the content is distributed.

2. Quantitative data related to or explaining how often the assessment includes the content against each criterion and across the criteria.

The first step to this tip is identifying what data you are using.

Assessment Tip #68
Authenticity

The rules of evidence identify the need to ensure assessments include the evidence that each assessment is completed by the student, meaning it is their own work that is presented. For observation and any other face-to-face methods of assessment this is easy; however, for methods such as online, this isn't as straightforward.

ASQA suggest calling the learner and asking questions relating to the assessment submitted or using the student's webcam to take photos of them at random intervals during the online assessment process. Other examples can be video submission of the student participating in the task and a declaration from them that it is their work. The holistic picture here is that even with assessment-only students, there is a need for all types and various methods of assessments to occur. This can include types such as formal, informal, summative, direct and supplementary.

Having more than one assessment occasion of interaction and connection assures the assessor that each assessment task has been completed by the student initially enrolled. They can be then be sure that this student's competency level is being measured. For example, only having a written theory or knowledge assessment will not show the student's competency in practically applying the task under assessment, nor will answering a set of questions after reading a case study provide evidence that the student's competency includes team work and collaboration skills. Different dimensions of competency must be considered for authentic evidence of competency to be achieved.

Assessment Tip #69
Comments

How can assessment feedback be helpful?

Assessment feedback or comments to the student can be just as important as the actual assessment evidence. The assessment process can be stressful, especially for those who have not sat or completed any assessments since school days. Terms for assessment in the vocational sector can include language such as exam, test or assignment.

For some, this language can have a significant impact on their confidence, reducing their self-belief and ability to achieve because they may not have done well in these 'types' of environments before. Some students need to be reassured that their understanding of the content is correct, making feedback extremely important to them. Some assessors, however, don't know what to write and go with the constantly used phrase of 'good work'. A statement of 'good work' doesn't provide much feedback nor enhance student confidence levels. Here are some suggestions of what more effective feedback should include:

🐾 Identify the strengths and weakness areas.

🐾 Identify specifically what, where and how to improve the skills and knowledge.

🐾 Note their level of improvement since the last assessment.

🐾 Assure that you are with them in their journey.

🐾 Use encouragement and constructive wording. If it is in person, I suggest demonstrating how the student can improve by showing them a different method/technique in the workplace task.

Assessment Tip #70
Workplace

What are workplace assessments?

Assessments that focus on equipping students for work are extremely powerful. Consider the impact that you, as an assessor, could have if the assessment process and activities were closely based on a real-world job situation. When this student then gets a job, they will be much more confident because they have already been in that same situation a number of times before.

Now consider how many theory questions you are making them write out, how many essays they have to write and how little opportunity the assessments give the students to collaborate, communicate and achieve real-world work goals.

Improve the assessment methods by asking in your next validation: Is the assessment process having an outcome of increasing student confidence? Is it reflective of what they will be doing on the job? Could the competent student walk into a workplace and do the job today? If yes, awesome. If no, fix this.

Assessment Tip #71
Data is Key

What data reflects assessment quality?

At the time this book was being created, I conducted a review of over 1.1 million fragments of content, taken from the statistics in the Prickly2sweet™ system. This table data identified the 10 most-used assessment methods. Specifically, this data identified the number of assessment types used in Australian VET during 2021–2022.

Top 10 assessment categories used and reviewed in the Prickly2sweet™ system during 2021–2022

Top 10	Type	Amount
1.	Written Knowledge Test, Short Answer, Essay	35,728
2.	Practical Demonstration	22,960
3.	Project/ Portfolio	9,033
4.	Competency Conversation	7,515
5.	Third Party Report	5,997
6.	Self-Assessment/ Reflection	4,520
7.	Summative Quiz, Multichoice	4,083
8.	Work Placement Observation	2,909
9.	Oral Presentation, interview, role play	2,238
10.	Formative Quiz, Multi-choice	2,118

The top 5 in-demand skills according to SEEK are highlighted below:

Emotional intelligence, technology literacy, resilience, agility and productivity.

What is so important about this type of research data? The data from Seek and Prickly2sweet™ shows the workplace skills needed and what is currently used as methods for skill assessment.

The Australian vocational sector needs to increase the methods of assessment that are using problem solving, resistance and agility, such as role plays, workplace observation and projects that are assessing proactivity. This means moving away from theory-only assessment. Projects could also be assessing technology skills, and self-assessment could be used for emotional intelligence.

TIP 1: Read the data and make the changes to assessment methods, types and evidence.

TIP 2: Use innovative ways to check your assessment against the unit criteria to make any improvement easier and ensure sufficient, reliable and valid assessment that shows students are competent.

Assessment Tip #72
Reasonable Adjustment

When should adjustment be considered?

Reasonable adjustment is about removing or reducing the effect of any disability so the students can complete assessments competently.

Adjustment is to be considered during all stages of training and assessment throughout the student's journey. Internally, make sure it is clear as to who is responsible for negotiating adjustments. Ensure they are aware of this role and have the professional skills and confidence to conduct the negotiation with the student and can implement the adjustments.

Lots of providers have reasonable adjustment statements in their marketing information and in their strategy; however, make sure you can support these should the need arise with records of negotiation and action of adjustments. Invite disclosure of the need to adjust well before assessment.

Assessment Tip #73
Practise Makes Perfect

'Practise makes perfect', but all of it does not have to be captured for the final assessment. Sufficient assessment evidence is when the assessor is assured that the quality, quantity and relevance of the assessment evidence enables a judgement to be made of a learner's competency.

Consider if the assessor is the trainer as well, as in most cases in an RTO. Practising techniques and competencies can be captured during training. During formative activities, capture role plays. During placements, this can be enhanced and assisted by others such as supervisors, team leaders and third parties. Clear assessment planning, criteria and evidence are key to compliance. Identify the points of final assessment, provide feedback for continual improvement and include opportunities for input from all stakeholders.

Be aware that the final judgement can only be completed by the qualified assessor. A competent assessor takes all the practice into account.

Assessment Tip #74
Creativity

> Where can you find innovative and creative assessment?

The creative assessment methods come from understanding your students. If you have a focus in your organisation such as an industry, deep dive into that industry. Research how they think, work and engage as a business, as well as what problems they have, and use this to design your assessment activities.

Innovation comes from seeing a problem within and finding a solution. Compliance training and assessment is one of those subjects close to my heart. Many find compliance training boring due to the need to be aware of specific legislation or compliance standards. Unfortunately, many have made compliance more boring than it needs to be. In fact, compliance training and assessment can be a lot of fun. A simple game of compliance bingo can be created, or a 'Guess Who?' game for vocational trainer and assessor requirements and currency. Assessment of problem solving and a compliance audit can be interactive using role plays and case studies. Self-reflection after a workplace audit and feedback can also assist in compliance skills and knowledge.

Assessment Tip #75
Pilot

What does it mean to 'pilot' assessment?

Piloting an assessment before you systemise an instrument is an opportunity to validate its efficiency and appropriateness. Piloting is when an assessment is tested in a small group before it is rolled out as the authorised version. This pilot process can include use by internal staff, previous students and industry employers.

When this occurs, please ensure the instructions to your stakeholders are clear on the purpose of the pilot and that you are collecting data on any improvements needed. Improvements can include effectiveness, current industry relevance, and authenticity of the activities, tasks and questions.

A pilot can be used for your validation process as well. Consider a scorecard approach against your RTO business values, resource allocation, performance indicators and industry outcome needs, as well as the unit requirements. Scorecards have been around in business for a while. For example, you can refer to 'A Better Scorecard: 3 Ways to Improve How Your Business Measures Success':

https://www.score.org/blog/better-scorecard-3-ways-improve-how-your-business-measures-success

Generally, these are used by businesses to measure their success against indicators such as customers, internal processes and finance. You can create a scorecard for specific areas of an RTO such as assessment design, development and validation.

TIP

Create a scorecard for your assessment pilot. Think of your overall compliance and quality goals in the RTO, then schedule the process to include weekly meetings so you and your team stay on top of completing the assessment and gathering that important feedback. Finally, set the metrics for data and outcome measurement. Focus on using the data in process improvement, such as design and format (linked to easy use and user satisfaction), such as

compliance with the unit (use a system that can give
you data of overall compliance).

Assessment Tip #76
Help

Can I ask for help?

Asking for help in assessment compliance is really fundamental to systematic improvement. Ensure you build a confident support team that knows the compliance requirements as well those who think outside the box. There are plenty of templates for assessment; however, you don't have to use them. You do not have to 'copy and paste' the unit before each assessment instrument or copy and paste each criterion as an objective of a task. You also do not have to write the unit criteria numbers against each question in the student or the assessor master.

It doesn't mean that if you do, it is wrong; it is just a waste of time. This is especially true when a unit or training package changes to include minor grammar amendments. This sort of change may not be picked up, or if it is, time is wasted to update the part of the assessment that does not have a huge impact on the tool.

Support and help could come from investing in making assessment compliance easier, along with making mapping and content review easy, quick and accurate. Help can also be investing in external support and assistance in compliance generally, or specific training in assessment methods and having a system in validation.

Assessment Tip #77
Wording

What wording should the assessment reflect?

Wording in the assessment should reflect the unit's terminology, context, intent and language. The key here is 'reflect' – do not copy and paste word-for-word sentences. For example, don't just drop in performance criteria as an observation task or as a benchmark response or suggested answer. Units use training-package language that outlines requirements. They are also written in a structure that is like a Lego instruction manual. You can't just put bits in; you must know how all the bits fit. This is where clear and holistic mapping makes all the difference. If the mapping for a unit is just the unit noting one criterion at a time in a sequential order, like it is presented in the unit, then is it really easy to think if you just copy the criteria into a task, it will cover the unit. The biggest mistake with this approach is that it doesn't consider the most important aspect of the vocational training and assessment: the student. A student does not do one criterion at a time; therefore, the assessment methods, tasks and questions should consider this perspective as well. Knowledge questions can be scaffolded to ensure the student builds on and provides evidence of their underpinning knowledge before the next assessment method.

In addition to this, the principles of assessment and rule of evidence are explained by the regulator:

'Ensure tasks for observation of a student's practical skills are well described and include observable behaviours. Do not, for example, simply cut and paste information from the unit of competency such as the performance criteria.'[22]

Assessment Tip #78
Insanity

Is it insanity or Déjà vu?

Assessment review and mapping has been done the same way for a long time, and it is producing the same bad outcome. Why are we as an industry expecting a different outcome? Assessment processes, tools and instruments will not improve if this continues as it hasn't improved for years. This is not only hurting the industry, but it is also hurting the students and the training organisations. The same mapping system is being taught in TAE, so nothing will change until this failure is learned from!

Flip this culture. Look for a new way of mapping to find a new outcome that is better for the students, the assessors and the RTO. What else is failing for the RTO as a business? What else should the team be learning from?

Assessment Tip #79
Reliable

Tired of the same methods all the time?

The continued use of the same assessment methods over and over for every unit of competency in a course or training product can be a quick way to reduce progression; for example, another set of knowledge questions, practical, and then a third party can get boring for assessors as well as students. Why not try a new assessment method? Let's use this tip as an opportunity to ask the community how they are assessing students.

Why not try role plays, case studies, projects or portfolios, or competency conversations? Learning is meant to be fun, and assessment can be as well. Create an assessment that they can use in the workplace once they get a job and can apply what they have learnt. Create something that can be either be taken with them, for example a portfolio, experience and/or an activity that they can remember.

Consider using technology, virtual or augmented reality, the latest equipment or method of production, testing or communication. Share the most memorable assessment you ever did.

My favourite ones at school were always things you could take home and share. As I got older and completed vocational courses, they were things like portfolios of production steps and flow charts that I used on other projects and shared with other staff. At university, the biggest assessment was a thesis that I fondly look back on with pride as it set me up for other business ventures.

Assessment Tip #80
Key

What are the assessment key must-haves?

A key assessment consideration is understanding that they have a few distinct purposes. So many times, I have heard people ask, 'Why can't the regulator just give us all a template or format to follow?'

I am of the belief that this would actually cause more harm than good. Obviously, all assessment must be compliant with the standards; however, the purpose, which we drill down into later, is actually not for audit or the regulator.

Let's for the moment consider this analogy. Without sounding too much like the Matrix, for a key to fit it has to be the same shape as the key hole. There are millions of key holes, some very similar but not the same. The same-looking door may also need a different key. Students are similar. The competency is the same as it is a standardised unit (same door); however, the students are very different – similar cohorts but different in competency behaviour.

These keys can have the same intent and process. This intent and process can be identified in a templated format of assessment tools with essentially the basic sections as noted in the documents such as 'Assessment in the VET Sector'. This includes the basics of names and signatures of participant, assessor, location and unit information – code and title, feedback, context, instructions, procedure, unit coverage and resources.

A lot of assessments miss key information, such as:

🐚 The difference between instructions for a participant compared to an assessor.

🐚 Consideration and reference to the whole assessment process and where the individual assessment sits in that sequence, for example task 2 of 3.

🐚 The ability for any variation, ability for confirmation with competency conversation, contextualisation.

🐚 Number of attempts for the participant.

🐚 Recording of any moderation process or use in moderation on the actual tool.

Assessment Tip #81
Related

What are related assessment activities?

All assessment points must be clearly articulated. This includes any resource and activities related to assessment. Like all compliant assessments, it has to meet the rules of evidence, principles of assessment and be conducted by a qualified assessor. Here is the key: Don't make this complicated!

🍍 Plan the process first, clearly identifying the type of evidence required for the unit. Do not just copy and paste the unit without thinking about the criteria alignment.

🍍 Strive for clear instructions to students and assessors about the process, documentation and records needed.

🐚 Be flexible with evidence-gathering methods and tools.

🐚 Report the outcome. Include feedback and the next step.

Assessment Tip #82
Complexity

Do assessments have to be complicated?

Stop making assessment so complicated.

Being prepared to conduct an assessment is one of the keys to successful assessments. How do you get prepared? Here are some tips:

🍍 Read the assessor marking guide/ or benchmark or assessor guide that meets the unit of competency.

🍍 Have all the equipment checked and set up ready to go.

🍍 Instruct the student the day before the process and of the expectation.

🍍 Review all the formative assessments for each student to determine any previous areas of lack of evidence in competency. These areas can be revisited in competency conversations naturally rather than being randomly introduced.

🍍 Make sure you have surveys for your students to complete at the end of the session.

🍍 Talk to your administration team and ensure all records are completed at the time of your student's participation.

Assessment Tip #83
Measurement

Are assessment objectives needed?

Assessment objectives are needed in your assessment instruments for students.

Objectives and goals are important in any process; however, just having an objective that outlines the criteria from the unit is not guaranteeing a compliant assessment. The intent of the assessment method, questions and tasks needs to reflect the strategy. If the steps in the assessment or the questions don't actually have that outcome and meet the objective, then it is pointless having the objective written in the document. [23]

TIP

Have only what you need in the instruments that the student uses and in the tools the assessor uses to guide the marking and judgement. Have everything else in the assessment process, strategy and planning documents. Having too much information can be as much of a problem as not having enough.

Always ask:

1. Why do we have this in here?

2. Do we need the document user to have this information?

Assessment Tip #84
RPL

Recognition of prior learning or RPL is defined in the AQF as 'an assessment process that involves assessment of an individual's relevant prior learning (including formal, informal and non-formal learning) to determine the credit outcomes of an individual application for credit.'[24]

Credit is the value assigned to recognise equivalence in content and learning outcomes between different types of learning and/or qualifications. Like all compliant assessment, it has to meet the rules of evidence, principles of assessment and be conducted by a qualified assessor. Here is the key: Don't make this complicated!

Rinse and Repeat

Step 1: Plan the process first, clearly identifying the type of evidence required for the unit. Do not copy and paste the unit without thinking about the alignment of the criteria.

Step 2: Strive for clear instructions to students and assessors about the process, documentation and records needed.

Step 3: Be flexible with evidence-gathering methods and tools.

Step 4: Report the outcome, including feedback and the next step.

Assessment Tip #85
Feedback

How much feedback does an assessor need to give in the assessments to pass audit? There are two areas to discuss here:

A The feedback areas designed in an assessment tool and system.

B The assessor's diligence in feedback completion. Please note the 'pass' audit is a variable that is not based on one section. For example, you could have a substantial amount of feedback and still not 'pass' audit because of other areas of noncompliance related to assessment.

So, my tips are:

🐚 Ensure feedback is given and recorded.

🐚 Ensure the assessment instruments don't have too much feedback, such as against each subsection task, that the assessor doesn't fill it in; otherwise, this will end up as non-compliance.

🐚 Provide feedback of the process, situation, skills and knowledge transfer confidence, areas for improvement and any other relevant areas that are appropriate and needed for and by the student. Don't just say good job!

🐚 Bonus points if you include references to further learning.

Assessment Tip #86
Outcome

As previously and initially noted in Tip #16, the outcome of an assessment is a reflection of the marking or assessment evidence. In this tip, the actual intended outcome of the assessment process rather than the activities will be looked at and commented on.

The learner or participant's motivation to complete the assessment, as well as the training, will probably be dependent on the original intent of starting it. For example, if the training was initiated to achieve a qualification, then the successful completion of the assessment is naturally required to achieve this outcome.

Similarly, as noted in the Tip #84 regarding RPL, although an assessment only processes the outcome of completing the at times long and arduous process, it is with the intended outcome of a qualification.

The need for a qualification can be varied. The variation can include the employment outcome requirement to get a job, keep a job or get a better a job. These are not the only reasons someone does an assessment in the vocational sector. Assessment may also be completed for self-motivated confidence boosters, life experience in a different field, such as those assessments needing hours of work in a placement situation, or just a self and lifelong learning activity to meet others and stay active.

The methods and types of assessment need to ensure these outcomes are met.[26] Have another look at TIP #83 regarding measurement to make sure what you are measuring for outcomes is aligned with the required assessment outcomes.

TIP

🐚 Ensure the assessment methods, tools and instruments reflect the specific intent of the person and/or cohort to determine whether the appropriate activities enable the required outcomes and find out more about your cohorts' needs.

Assessment Tip #87
Attempts

There is no set number of times needed or required to be deemed competent in an assessment activity. There is no official requirement; however, there is an element of 'fairness' for the participant as well as for the RTO. Investigating the reason for subsequent attempts is just as important as it provides opportunities for additional competent outcomes.

Furthermore, there should be evidence that if throughout the assessment process there are signs of a challenge or lack of understanding, then additional learning opportunities rather than a failed assessment are provided.

Assessment Tip #88
Purpose

What are the assessment key purposes?

As previously and initially noted in Tip #16, the outcome of an assessment is a reflection of the marking or assessment evidence. In this tip, the actual intended outcome of the assessment process rather than the activities' assessments has a few purposes.

As noted previously in TIP #80, assessments need to be compliant with the national standards; however, the purpose is to gather and collate evidence of a student's competency to enable an assessor to form a judgement of their skills and knowledge for a particular unit or set of units. This evidence, summative and formative, provides the picture and history of assessment activities. The purpose will include all the requirements and key information. The assessment purpose is the same, but the method of assessment processes, assessment tools and strategy will all be different and reflect the needs of both industry and the students/cohort of student characteristics and needs.

Assessment Tip #89
Accessible

One of the principles outlined by Jisc in 2020, which is also embedded as part of the national standards for RTOs in Australia is that the accessibility of assessment encompasses access, equity and responsiveness to individual needs.[26]

Assessment accessibility needs to start at the design of assessment. It also must be included in the strategy of the practice and processes, and contain the methods and distribution platform, information, instruction and collation of competency evidence. Mary Burns noted that 'Technology cannot make a poorly designed assessment better; it just scales a poorly designed assessment to more people'.[27]

The Covid-19 pandemic has led to a necessary increase in speed of change. A large portion of this change has been to pivot previously designed face-to-face assessments into an online platform of distribution. Although intended to make training and assessment more accessible, it has actually led to a decrease in accessibility. This outcome has been due to retrofitting content or trying to use what was already available and tack it on rather than redesigning it for the modality. Accessibility in this case is not only for those who self-identify as having a disability but for all participants who work well in a face-to-face environment who could now be disadvantaged in the online environment.

Assessment accessibility needs to consider the platform it is being distributed and accessed from, as well as the content and context to ensure the tasks and delivery are appropriate for the participant and the topic. Similar to offline assessment, online assessment has to meet the principles of assessment and rules of evidence. Online has another set of criteria to consider and that is the interaction/action of the participant to either select or construct a response online.

Assessment provides a range of ways for individuals to demonstrate that they have met the required outcomes of the unit and can be granted recognition of competency levels. RPL is basically a mapping of learning outcome evidence from prior learning evidence and activities to the qualification and specific unit components.

Assessment Tip #90
Insufficient Files

How do you deal with insufficient files? Records management is part of a quality system no matter if you are an RTO or if you are a business in any sector. A lack of files makes your job much harder. If you are the recipient in this situation, here are some tips to get the assessment evidence back on track:

🍍 Know your unit and know what you need to obtain for evidence of competency.

🍍 Pinpoint the record and missing evidence gaps.

🍍 Look at a training and assessment plan for the student and the strategy for the course to identify opportunities for gathering the missing evidence.

🐚 Communicate the need for more evidence with the student as well as the RTO team/supervisor/team leader/employer.

🐚 Create a competency conversation to capture the missing evidence.

🐚 Ensure the root cause of the problem is fixed so that systemically it doesn't happen again and all other gaps can be actioned.

🐚 Record the improvement.

Assessment Tip #91
Not One for One

You don't have to do one question/task for each criterion. When you are reviewing your assessment and using a mapping document or matrix, are you looking from the point of the assessment method to the unit or the unit criteria to the assessment?

If you are looking from the criteria, say knowledge evidence, you don't have to see another or separate assessment question or task or evidence. If your mapping has been or is being completed manually, the format dictates that you must have one assessment for each criterion, one at a time. It is the way the brain is reading the unit and the way the mapping is structured that makes you think it has to be done this way. This is mainly because this format method lists each criterion separately from the other criterion it is related to. First thing – STOP! Second, measure how much time this is wasting. Most knowledge evidence is linked to performance criteria and/or performance evidence.

Too many assessments are written to the criteria, so they end up being massive and repetitive because they fail to see the unit criteria links and relationships. Not to mention there is no reflection of an actual task in the workplace. If you create the assessment to meet the student and workplace needs and then identify how it meets one or more units, you will get a much higher-quality assessment. Use a system that focuses on the task.

Remember to align the criteria first inside the unit, thinking about how the learner would holistically complete the task.

Assessment Tip #92
Learner Cohort

Quality assessment considers, and is designed to meet, the needs of the learner cohort. Here are some tips to work out who your learner cohort is. Ask the following questions:

Do they have:

🍍 Language, literacy and numeracy needs – consider observation assessment, additional support and practical assessment.

🍍 Workplace experience/working/not working – if they have some experience then use a case study assessment, on-the-job assessment and supplementary third-party supervisor reports of experience.

🐾 Personal characteristics – ages, gender association, education levels, motivation and cultural backgrounds.

🐾 Readiness to learn and grow.

🐾 Alignment and aspiration with the qualification and/or unit description; for example, they aspire to operational roles, generally work under minimal supervision to undertake a broad range of tasks in varied work contexts and use some discretion and judgement in selecting equipment, services or contingency measures.

Tips 4 and 5 are usually missed in cohort awareness and are not measured or captured. It should be the basis of the industry engagement.

BONUS Tip: All of the above should be clearly identified in your training and assessment strategy.

Assessment Tip #93
Third Party

What does third party mean?

There are two types of third parties. One is third-party evidence, which is different to third-party assessment arrangements.

🍍 Third-party EVIDENCE is supplementary evidence and/or additional evidence presented to assessors to support a candidate's claim of competence. This includes reports from supervisors, colleagues and/or clients, testimonials from employers, work diaries and training evidence.

🍍 Third-party ARRANGEMENTS are when other organisations (third parties) work with an RTO to deliver a range of services, including providing marketing, undertaking recruitment, using facilities and resources, and training and/or assessment of VET courses.

The first one is easy, but the second one is more complex because it is full of compliance pitfalls. It also needs management, monitoring and documentation and cannot be used for all qualifications.

TIP

Visit the ASQA website where you will find fact sheets and clear information on what is needed.

Under the Australian accredited and nationally recognised system, only an assessor compliant with the standards, including clauses noting the compliance of an RTO, is the one who can make a judgement of competency based on assessment evidence.

ASQA has noted the common reasons an RTO would use another party for the process of gathering evidence such as:

🐾 The presence of an observer may compromise workplace safety, or

🐾 Where work activities involve issues of patient confidentiality and privacy.[28]

Assessment Tip #94
Co-assessment

What is co-assessment?

I have been working in Australia's vocational sector for over twenty years, and this is a new term for me. 'Co-assessment arrangement,' according to ASQA is 'when an assessor, qualified and compliant with the national standards, and another party work together to conduct assessment.'[29]

Under clauses 1.13 and 1.14 of the Standards for RTOs it is acceptable for an industry expert to both conduct the assessment and be involved in the assessment judgement. This is a great idea as long as it is clear who is qualified for what part of the process, and yes, this needs to be in a formal agreement. It is still the qualified assessor, with the TAE components, who does the final sign-off.[30]

The best practice model for co-assessing includes the following:

A guide or internal standards must identify who this co-assessor should be. The guide is to include how the co-assessment process works and who is responsible for what part of the assessment. It is important to ensure the co-assessor understands and provides confirmation that they agree to the process. Another important aspect of the guide includes the interpretation agreement of the unit of competency, including what a competent behaviour, practice, knowledge application looks like. Benchmark responses in a trainer and assessor guide or similar for each assessment task and question assists with this clarification. Agreement should be included in validation meetings and confirmed when students' completed work is included in the validation sample.

Finally, it has to include all aspects related to evidence. This includes HOW, WHEN, WHERE, WHY, WHO. These incorporate all standard requirements of the assessment, including all the other rules of evidence as required for any assessment, such as benchmarks and assessor guides.

Co-Assessor Guide Content

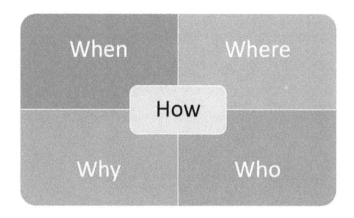

BONUS TIP

Written agreements, benchmarks and the skills matrix of all assessors assist with the evidence of the arrangement as well as in the management and performance of the co-assessing arrangements. Summary of TIP #94 includes having:

🐚 written agreements of all co-assessment arrangements.

🐚 a matrix of assessors.

🐚 evidence of compliance with the RTO standards for assessors.

🐚 benchmark/assessor guides clearly identifying what competency is and what evidence would be acceptable.

Assessment Tip #95
Planning Importance

Why is assess-
ment panning
crucial?

I have experienced, seen and heard from a lot of assessors in situations where they are 'given' the assessment kit and tools and are expected to 'run with it'. You hope before this point that there has been some planning involved, some analysis of the cohort, some organisation strategy and some prior-to-use validation. If this is your experience, you have evidence of all this and have reviewed your assessment for your own professional and ethical values and are happy with it – Awesome! If everything mentioned after 'run with it' hasn't been done, or there is no evidence, then now is your time as a qualified assessor to make your mark and actually plan it out. Don't wait for someone else to do it.

Key aspects of the importance of planning include:

🐾 Plan the assessment to be meaningful, manageable, measurable and sustainable.

🐾 Ensure the plan includes the end goal; for example, transference of skills and knowledge for a workplace task and job.

🐾 Include others so everyone knows the plan and why the assessment is what it is. Better still, chat to your compliance person and see them smile and maybe even cry with gratitude.

Assessment Tip #96
Assessment System

'An assessment system includes not only the actual materials used directly in conducting assessment, but also policies, procedures and other supporting documents and tools that inform the way assessment is conducted within your RTOs.'[31] This is particularly important for the validation process; however, understanding the system of assessment is also important for all involved from planners, designers and facilitators to compliance. The full assessment system is to include all points of assessment. For example, a self-assessment and learner-needs discussion before training, monitoring progression with formative assessment and summative assessment activities at the end of training. It also includes contextualisation processes, feedback evidence, workplace and industry engagement and human re-source processes for assessors.

TIP

Have a visual chart of what this looks like, an organi-sation structure, and identify the flow of the student's journey and the points of reference.

Assessment Tip #97
Technology

Is technology just a learner management system (LMS)?

As mentioned previously, Mary Burns highlighted that 'technology cannot make a poorly designed assessment better—it just scales a poorly designed assessment to more people.'[32]

Considering that Covid led to a necessary speed of change for a large portion of previously designed face-to-face assessments, our industry has been pushed into an online platform of distribution. This may have led to a decrease in accessibility just for the fact that assessments have been retrofitted or RTOs have tried to use what they had and tack it on rather than redesign it for the modality.

Accessibility in this case is not only for those who self-identify as having a disability but also for participants who work well in a face-to-face environment, who could now be disadvantaged in the online environment.

TIP

Assessment accessibility needs to consider the platform it is being distributed and accessed from, as well as the content and context to ensure the tasks and delivery is appropriate for the participant and the topic. As with offline assessment, online assessment has to meet the principles of assessment and rules of evidence.

Online assessment has another set of criteria to consider and that is the screen interaction/action of the participant to either select or construct a response online.

Assessment Tip #98
Internal Controls

What can you use internal control checks for?

Internal control checks after assessments have been completed is the final piece of the puzzle for RTOs before issuing certificates or statements of attainment. This is particularly important for those organisations that have multiple assessors, assessment methods and administration staff.

It is a team effort to ensure all the 'i's are dotted and 't's crossed. Providers must have a documented and clear process that is followed by the whole organisation to prevent final certification from being issued and noted in the leaner management system (LMS) until all required assessments have been completed and all evidence has been obtained. This can include work placement, specific practical days and final discussions with supervisors in the workplace. Additionally, RTOs must ensure that all assessments have been checked for complete marking, feedback, signatures and dates. This may include final authenticity checks and moderation across assessors.

There are plenty of other compliance requirements related to issuing certificates, including within 30 days of final assessment noted as completed and competent.

Assessment Tip #99
Records Management

What are the key areas for records management?

Assessment records management can be very simple. It is critical to maintain evidence of the student's completed assessments. This includes 'the actual piece(s) of work completed by a student or evidence of that work, including evidence collected for an RPL process. An assessor's completed marking guide, criteria and observation checklist for each student may be sufficient where it is not possible to retain the student's actual work. However, the retained evidence must have enough detail to demonstrate the assessor's judgement of the student's performance against the standard required.' [33]

Records mean a written, printed or electronic document providing evidence that activities have been performed.

Here are the key things to remember:

At 6 months from the date of judgement, each student's completed assessment items must be maintained. Other contracts and licencing requirements may require longer retention of the actual assessment documents.

Thirty years after the completion date and certificate or statement of attainment has been issued, retain the records of outcomes, which includes a register of all the AQF qualifications and statement of attainments (SOAs) that have been issued. Refer to the standards for all other recording requirements such as validation.

Assessment Tip #100
Deficient

What makes an assessment deficient?

Deficient assessments due to poor design can be a situation that many assessors face. Here are 4 things you can do:

🐚 Identify the deficiencies and note them on the mapping document. Remember the mapping document was supposed to be designed to identify how the assessment system meets the unit, so if you find something isn't covered, identify the problem.

🐚 Create a solution. This might be as simple as documenting a competency conversation with the student on the areas not yet covered in the other assessments.

🐚 Communicate both the issue and solution to the team, other assessors, compliance and team leader, or whoever it is in your organisation that needs to know.

🐚 Validate the tools and invest in an updated method of assessment review to identify other gaps, which will be more accurate and better for all stakeholders. This process will also include samples of other students to deal with any other the bigger or systemic issues to be addressed.

Assessment Tip #101
Compliance

What is the final tip?

For the final tip there is an overall question to ask: Is the assessment compliant?

It is not that there is a secret way of checking assessments as there are clear requirements for the validation process. Assessment compliance is a complex, holistic process that needs to check all the principles of assessment and rules of evidence. Assessment methods, tools and instruments should be piloted, moderated and validated. Everyone should be included at specific times that are relevant both to them and the assessment system. The system is the key to compliance. A system needs to be efficient, effective, measured and manageable. My final tip is to automate where you can, while management of the organisation needs to include risk awareness and governance of the assessment system.

Like any complex compliance requirement, if you break it down into specific pieces, it will be easier to identify trends in compliance issues, investigate the source of the problems and conduct rectification for improvement in quality and compliance.

If you are in the business of vocational education in Australia and want to responsibly issue qualifications, certificates and statements of attainment, compliance in assessment is one of the key areas to manage well as it has the biggest impact on the level of quality in individual industries.

With all these 101 tips, I hope you have a better understanding of the vocational assessment sector, and I wish all my readers the very best in assessment compliance and all aspects of quality training and assessment.

Acknowledgements

I would like to acknowledge and thank some amazing people who have helped me create this book.

Alivia Clark, an amazing young artist who created the character Prickly, our little pineapple friend that asks all the questions throughout this book for us.

My family, specifically Dave and Connor, for helping me to set aside the time for this creation, along with all the encouragement and ideas.

My family (team) at Prickly2sweet™ – Rachel, Ryan, and Isabella – for working hard on keeping the business going.

Julie Edwards, for all the reviews of content and comments. It was really appreciated.

Dr Juliette Lachemeier, my fantastic editor and independent publisher at The Erudite Pen.

ABOUT THE AUTHOR

Vanessa McCarthy has over 20 years' experience in the vocational education and training sector within a wide variety of compliance roles, where she specialises in assessment compliance.

As a strategic thinker, Vanessa makes things happen, and she can get ideas come to life. She takes charge, speaks up and makes sure others are heard. She builds strong relationships that hold a team together. Vanessa's ability to absorb and analyse information enables her to make informed decisions, which helps her to deal with complex compliance issues in assessment. She strives to provide information about assessment to inspire and push others to new heights of quality, excellence and compliance.

Vanessa is passionate and dedicated to quality in vocational education, especially assessment and validation processes. An innovator, small business and company owner, director and entrepreneur, she currently works in assessment review and RTO compliance.

Being committed to compliance innovation and system improvement in VET, Vanessa created Valid8ed™ and Prickly2sweet™. These comprise the first online assessment review system that maps and gap analyses assessment resources. The system then provides clear and measurable data on compliance, as well as reports that are easy to read and useful in improvement, down to the keyword.

Vanessa lives in Cairns with her husband Dave and is a proud mum of two young men. She has been the managing director of her own business since 2015, has a Bachelor of Applied Science, multiple diplomas and an Advanced Diploma in Education.

Enjoyed the book? You can follow Vanessa McCarthy at:

Website: prickly2sweet.com.au/

Facebook: www.facebook.com/Prickly2sweet

LinkedIn: www.linkedin.com/company/valid8ed/

If you enjoyed the book, please leave a review on the author's social media pages, your own media pages, Amazon or Goodreads etc. This support is greatly appreciated by all authors.

Endnotes

1. Caroline Garaway, "How we raised our NSS feedback and assessment scores by 26% in three years," UCL, accessed January 11, 2022, https://www.ucl.ac.uk/teaching-learning/case-studies/2018/apr/how-we-raised-our-nss-feedback-and-assessment-scores-26-three-years.

2. "Clauses 1.22 to 1.24 – Employ experts to teach trainers and assessors," Chapter 4 – Training and assessment, ASQA, accessed November 22, 2021, https://www.asqa.gov.au/rtos/users-guide-standards-rtos-2015/chapter-4-training-and-assessment/clauses-122-124-employ-experts-teach-trainers-and-assessors.

3. "Appendix 7: Rules of evidence," Accredited courses guide appendices, ASQA, accessed December, 3, 2022, https://www.asqa.gov.au/course-accreditation/users-guide-standards-vet-accredited-courses/accredited-courses-guide-appendices/appendix-7-rules-evidence.

4. "Standard 10.12 – Course Assessment Strategy," Standards, ASQA, accessed March 15, 2022, https://www.asqa.gov.au/course-accreditation/users-guide-standards-vet-accredited-courses/standards/standard-1012-course-assessment-strategy.

5. "Appendix 7: Rules of evidence," Accredited courses guide appendices, ASQA, accessed December, 3, 2022, https://www.asqa.gov.au/course-accreditation/users-guide-standards-

vet-accredited-courses/accredited-courses-guide-appendices/appendix-7-rules-evidence.

6. "CHCECE007 – Develop positive and respectful relationships with children," Details, Training.gov.au, accessed October 20, 2021, https://training.gov.au/Training/Details/CHCECE007.

7. ACT Government Education, Teachers' Guide to Assessment, (Canberra: Education ACT, 2016), Introduction, 6, https://www.education.act.gov.au/__data/assets/pdf_file/0011/297182/Teachers-Guide-To-Assessment.pdf.

8. "Standard 10.2 and 10.3 – Enterprise units of competency," Standards, ASQA, accessed July 10, 2021, https://www.asqa.gov.au/course-accreditation/users-guide-standards-vet-accredited-courses/standards/standard-102-and-103-enterprise-units-competency.

9. "Details - Performance Criteria 4.2 and 4.3," taeass401, training.gov.au. accessed 30 August 2021, https://training.gov.au/training/details/taeass401.

10. "What evidence do I need to demonstrate I have engaged with industry? What is meant by "range of strategies for industry engagement? (Clauses 1.5 – 1.6)," FAQs, ASQA, accessed July 15, 2021, https://www.asqa.gov.au/faqs/what-evidence-do-i-need-demonstrate-i-have-engaged-industry-what-meant-range-strategies.

11. National Quality Council (NQC), Evaluation of the Training Package development and endorsement process: final report (Melbourne: NQC Secretariat, 2009), https://www.voced.edu.au/content/ngv%3A32951.

12. National Quality Council (NQC), "A Code of Professional Practice for Validation and Moderation", accessed August, 10, 2021, https://www.ncver.edu.au.

13. National Quality Council (NQC), A code of professional practice for validation and moderation (Melbourne: TVET Australia, 2009), https://www.voced.edu.au/content/ngv%3A54572.

14. National Quality Council (NQC), A code of professional practice for validation and moderation (Melbourne: TVET Australia, 2009), https://www.voced.edu.au/content/ngv%3A54572.

15. National Quality Council (NQC), A code of professional practice for validation and moderation (Melbourne: TVET Australia, 2009), https://www.voced.edu.au/content/ngv%3A54572.

16. National Quality Council (NQC), A code of professional practice for validation and moderation (Melbourne: TVET Australia, 2009), https://ontargetworkskills.files.wordpress.com/2019/03/2009-nqc-validation-and-moderation-code-of-professional-practice.pdf.

17. National Quality Council (NQC), A code of professional practice for validation and moderation (Melbourne: TVET Australia, 2009), https://ontargetworkskills.files.wordpress.com/2019/03/2009-nqc-validation-and-moderation-code-of-professional-practice.pdf.

18. Josie Misko and Sian Halliday-Waynes, Assessment issues in VET: minimising the level of risk (Adelaide: NCVER, 2013).

19. "Standard 10.2 and 10.3 – Enterprise units of competency," Standards, ASQA, accessed July 10, 2021, https://www.asqa.gov.au/course-accreditation/users-guide-standards-vet-accredited-courses/standards/standard-102-and-103-enterprise-units-competency.

20. "Policy making at a distance: a critical perspective on Australia's National Foundation Skills Strategy for Adults", VOCED plus, accessed 11, September, 2021,
https://www.voced.edu.au/search/site/text%3A%28Strategy%20for%20adults%29

21. "Designing assessment tools for quality outcomes in VET", VOCED plus, accessed 11, September, 2021,
https://www.voced.edu.au/content/ngv%3A65904

22. "Clauses 1.8 to 1.12—Conduct Effective Assessment," Chapter 4 training and assessment, ASQA, accessed October 15, 2021,
https://www.asqa.gov.au/rtos/users-guide-standards-rtos-2015/chapter-4-training-and-assessment/clauses-18-112-conduct-effective-assessment.

23. Donald L. Kirkpatrick and James D. Kirkpatrick, Evaluating Training Programs: The Four Levels, 3rd Ed.(California: Berrett-Koehler, 2006), 245.

24. "Recognition of Prior Learning," Standards, FAQS, ASQA, accessed July 10, 2021, https://www.asqa.gov.au/standards/faqs/recognition-prior-learning

25. "The Assessment Purpose Triangle: Balancing the Purposes of Educational Assessment", Frontiers,
https://www.frontiersin.org/articles/10.3389/feduc.2017.00041/full

26. Duncan Borman et.al., "The future of assessment: five principles, five targets for 2025," Jisc, Spring 2020,
https://repository.jisc.ac.uk/7733/1/the-future-of-assessment-report.pdf

27. Mary Burns, "Developing Good Online Assessments Guidelines," elearningindustry.com, accessed (2021),
https://elearningindustry.com/developing-good-online-assessments-guidelines

28. "Standard 10.2 and 10.3 – Enterprise units of competency," Standards, ASQA, accessed July 10, 2021, https://www.asqa.gov.au/course-accreditation/users-guide-standards-vet-accredited-courses/standards/standard-102-and-103-enterprise-units-competency.

29. "Guide to using other parties to collect assessment evidence," ASQA, accessed October, 23, 2021, https://www.asqa.gov.au/guide-using-other-parties-collect-assessment-evidence

30. Ibid

31. "Standard 10.2 and 10.3 – Enterprise units of competency," Standards, ASQA, accessed July 10, 2021, https://www.asqa.gov.au/course-accreditation/users-guide-standards-vet-accredited-courses/standards/standard-102-and-103-enterprise-units-competency.

32. Mary Burns, "Developing Good Online Assessments Guidelines," elearningindustry.com, accessed (2021), https://elearningindustry.com/developing-good-online-assessments-guidelines

33. "Standard 10.2 and 10.3 – Enterprise units of competency," Standards, ASQA, accessed July 10, 2021, https://www.asqa.gov.au/course-accreditation/users-guide-standards-vet-accredited-courses/standards/standard-102-and-103-enterprise-units-competency.

CPSIA information can be obtained
at www.ICGtesting.com
Printed in the USA
BVHW012128300123
657453BV00015B/152